Book plus "Taliesin Insert"

FRANK LLOYD
WRIGHT

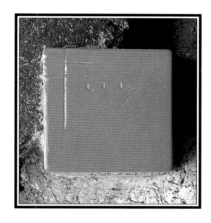

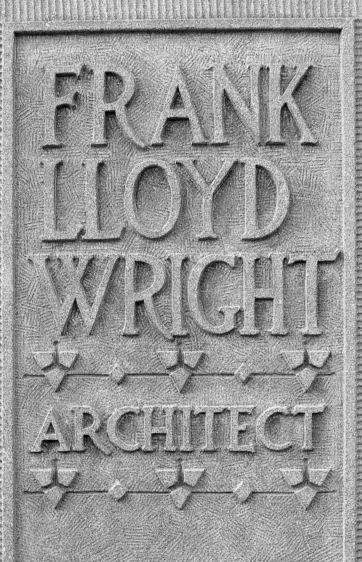

FRANK LLOYD
WRIGHT

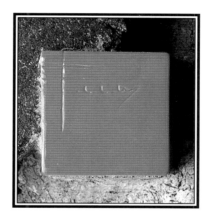

IAIN THOMSON

THUNDER BAY
P·R·E·S·S

The Introduction was written by Sandra Forty.
The Interior Designs chapter was written by Doreen Ehrlich.
All the photography except where credited below was by Simon Clay.

This edition published in 1997 by
Thunder Bay Press
5880 Oberlin Drive, Suite 400
San Diego, California 92121
1-800-284-3580

http://www.adms.web.com

Produced by the
Promotional Reprint Company Ltd,
Kiln House, 210 New Kings Road, London SW6 4NZ

Copyright © 1997 Promotional Reprint Company Ltd

ISBN 1 57145 134 X

Printed and bound in China

PAGE 1 and 3: Frank Lloyd Wright signature tile
from the First Christian Church, Phoenix, Arizona.

PAGE 2: Carved stone on front of Wright's Oak Park home.

*The Publisher would like to thank all the house owners and organizations that
allowed us access to their premises; and would particularly like to thank the
following people and organizations for their generosity and time
in helping to compile the book.*

1st National Bank of Dwight	Mildred Rosenbaum
Allice Shaddle	Mr & Mrs G Ablin
Arizona State University	Mr & Mrs J Howlett
for permission to photograph the	Mrs R Berger
Grady Gamage Memorial Auditoriam	Phillips Petroleum
Augustus Brown-Charles Ennis House	Photograph on page 114 by Matt Phalen
Bert Boyle	The Allen Lambe Study Centre
County of Marin Office	The Arizona Biltmore Hotel
of the Adminstrator –	The Barton House
Elizabeth Suki Sennet and Martin J Nichols	The Beth Sholom Synagogue
Daryle Smirl	The Carnegie Museum of Art
Don & Virginia Lovness	The Community Christian Church
Donald P Hallmark	The Dallas Theatre Centre
Dr R E McCoy	The Danna Thomas House
First Christian Church	The Fabian Villa
Florida Southern College	The Fasbender Medical Centre
Frank Lloyd Wright Foundation Taliesen East	The Hollyhock House
Frank Lloyd Wright Foundation Taliesen West	The Lowell Walter House
Frank Lloyd Wright Home & Studio Jean L. Guarino	The Pilgrim Congretional Church
Herman Hershman	The Pope Leighey House
Howard Ellington	The Society of Architectural Historians
Jack Larson	The Unitarian Meeting House
Jim Cavadis	The Unity Temple
Johnsons Wax	The Zimmerman House
Lisa Dodge	Todd C Barton
Louis J Frank	Whichita State University

While every attempt has been made to ensure the accuracy of this work, a project of this nature will always require updating and correction. The Publisher
welcomes comments for use in the preparation of the next edition.

CONTENTS

INTRODUCTION 6

FRANK LLOYD WRIGHT STATE-BY-STATE

ALABAMA. 18

ARIZONA. 20

CALIFORNIA 32

CONNECTICUT. .60

DELAWARE. 60

FLORIDA. 62

IDAHO 68

INDIANA. 68

ILLINOIS 70

IOWA. 112

KANSAS 120

KENTUCKY. 128

MARYLAND. 128

MASSACHUSETTS. 129

MICHIGAN 129

MINNESOTA 136

MISSOURI 142

MISSISSIPPI 143

MONTANA. 144

NEBRASKA. 145

NEW HAMPSHIRE. 146

NEW JERSEY 150

NEW MEXICO 151

NEW YORK. 152

OHIO 162

OKLAHOMA 164

OREGON 166

PENNSYLVANIA. 168

SOUTH CAROLINA 173

TENNESSEE. 173

TEXAS 174

VIRGINIA 178

WASHINGTON 183

WISCONSIN 184

WYOMING 195

**THE INTERIOR DESIGNS OF FRANK LLOYD
WRIGHT**. 196

DEMOLISHED BUILDINGS 246

CHRONOLOGY .250

INDEX 254

INTRODUCTION

Frank Lloyd Wright in 1903.

Frank Lloyd Wright was indisputably one of the greatest and most influential architects of the twentieth century. His reputation took time to grow and his achievements were first applauded abroad, principally in Germany, before his countrymen recognized his innovative significance. His long career of over 70 years encompassed modern technological developments in both building materials and techniques and Frank Lloyd Wright was one of the first architects to explore and exploit the new opportunities that these exciting technological developments made possible.

Inevitably, over such a span, many of his plans never saw fruition and remained unbuilt, but he left behind extensive writings and drawings, explaining and illuminating his ideas so that his thoughts at least are not lost to posterity. Unusually, perhaps, for such a great architect, much of his most significant and innovative work was domestic, and no example of his genius remains outside the United States, besides a house in Canada, two residences, a girls' school and a fragment of the lobby of the demolished Imperial Hotel in Japan, and a rebuilt office in the Victoria and Albert Museum, London. His work is also surprisingly parochial, fully two-thirds of the buildings he designed are in the midwest — 88 in Illinois and 43 in Wisconsin.

From a distance it seems that Wright spent much of his life embroiled in controversy: from the quarrels within his own family between his parents, the emotional conflicts he brought on himself by abandoning his wife and mother of his six children for another married woman, his noisy pacifism during the war which brought him many new enemies, not to mention his anti-establishment stance towards fellow architects, other people's architecture, planning regulations as well as bureaucracy and society in general. Always arrogant and disinclined to listen to the opinion of others, Frank Lloyd Wright, while able to make enemies with ease, also made strong friendships and inspired tremendous loyalty from his followers.

Frank Lloyd Wright was born to his father's second wife, Anna Lloyd Jones, on June 8, 1867, at Richland Center, Wisconsin. Right from the start she championed his cause to the detriment of everyone else, especially her husband, and even her two subsequent daughters. Frank's father, William Cary Wright, was a New Englander from a family of nonconformists who had emigrated from England early on in the seventeenth century. He earned his living as a music teacher and traveling Baptist minister, until he finally settled his wife and three children at Lone Rock, Wisconsin. Money, as ever, was tight so they took in boarders, one of whom was Anna Lloyd Jones a schoolteacher of God-fearing Unitarian Welsh stock whose wealthy land-owning family lived in Spring Green, Wisconsin.

When William was widowed in 1864 at age 44, Anna made up her mind to marry him; after all he was an attractive and intelligent man and a good catch for a strong-willed, plain, 29-year-old woman already considered over the hill by her family. Two years later, despite the age gap and their religious chasm, her family reluctantly agreed to their marriage. Within ten months baby Frank Lloyd Wright was born; two years later, in 1869, Jane arrived, and then nine years later, Maginel.

Sadly, the marriage was not a success: there was no meeting of minds — William cared only for music and Anna for education, specifically her son's education. She drilled into him her Unitarian values of faith in the family and a general liberal philosophy towards life. In 1876 an important, possibly life-changing, influence was experienced by the young Frank Lloyd Wright. His mother went to the Centennial Exhibition in Philadelphia. Here his mother was enthused with the ideas of the great German educationalist, Friedrich W. A. Froebel. As part of his thinking he developed the kindergarten system for very young children and, more pertinently for Frank and his mother, had developed a system of games which involved putting together simple, primary color, geometric shapes to make imaginative constructions. They were, in essence, building blocks. In his autobiography Wright claimed that these simple "toys" (as Froebel called them) were deeply influential to his architectural work.

Back in Wisconsin the following year, relations between his parents disintegrated further. Anna disliked her step-children and sent them away, and Frank had little further contact with them. Instead he got to know his cousins when he and his sister spent the summers on his uncle James Lloyd Jones's farm in Spring Green. Here, although he hated the holidays, he found in himself a interest in nature and the feel of the land.

His father left home when Wright was 18 and eventually divorced Anna. This left Wright completely under the influence of his fearsome mother, so much so that he became increasingly estranged from his father, even to the extent that he didn't attend his funeral.

Despite his mother's intensive educational ideas and promptings, Wright failed to graduate high school and in 1885 became apprenticed to the only builder in Madison, Allan D. Conover. As luck would have it, Conover was also dean of engineering at the University of Wisconsin, and he allowed his young apprentice to attend classes in the department of engineering. Here Wright received the only strict training he got of any sort — in draftsmanship; at the same time he was getting practical building experience in the office. The two years of classes he had before he dropped out showed that the young Frank Lloyd Wright had a remarkable ability for draftsmanship.

In 1887 Wright moved to Chicago. He was now 20 years old and moving to one of the most exciting cities in the United States. Devastated in 1871 by a great fire, it was only really now recovering and rebuilding fully. Architects and designers from all over America, especially the eastern seaboard, were arriving to take up the golden architectural opportunity this presented. Notable among these men was Joseph Lyman Silsbee, a much sought-after architect of mainly residential buildings in the

ABOVE: Louis Sullivan, Wright's mentor and a great influence on Wright's decorative style.

BELOW: Carving from the Charnley House, 1365 Astor, Chicago.

Norman Shaw "Shingle Style." Wright had an easy introduction to him as at the time Silsbee was working on a new building for All Souls' Church where his uncle, the Reverend Jenkin Lloyd Jones, was pastor. In spring 1887 Silsbee took on Wright as an apprentice and allowed him to do a little work on the church.

Still living with his mother and sisters who had moved to Chicago to be with him, Wright started reading voraciously. The anti-establishment stance of John Ruskin, the social theorist and greatest English art and architecture critic of his time (he had championed the Pre-Raphaelites' cause) appealed to Frank, as did the progressive ideas of the Arts and Crafts movement led by William Morris. As for work, he rapidly became bored with the "safe" architecture of Silsbee's practice and in the fall of the same year moved on to work for the firm of Adler and Sullivan. Their progressive style was much more to his taste, and in the end Wright stayed for six years. Louis Sullivan was a 31-year-old Bostonian and already a noted architect, considered by many to be the greatest American architect of the time. His epigram "form follows function" came also to be at the heart of Wright's work. Very soon Sullivan was to design and build the world's first skyscraper, the Wainwright Building in St. Louis, Missouri.

Frank Lloyd Wright quickly settled into the firm and in 1889 signed a five-year contract. By this time he was given the majority of the domestic commissions that came to the firm as the principals worked on their larger, public commissions, and the following year he took sole responsibility for all domestic work handled by the firm. Wright greatly admired Sullivan, whom he came to call his *Lieber Meister,* and was further influenced by Sullivan's personal interest in and collection of "Orientalia".

Around this time Wright met and soon married Catherine Lee Tobin, the daughter of a successful Chicago businessman. For their home he purchased the plot of land in Forest Avenue, Oak Park, next door to the house he shared with his mother and sisters. With $5,000 advanced by Sullivan he set about designing and building a six-room bungalow. The building shows the influence of the "*Lieber Meister*" and other eastern seaboard architects such as Richardson. In common with all his houses throughout his life, this was only the beginning of continuous re-designs and rebuilding.

In 1893 Frank was exposed to two more crucial influences on his development as an architect, when the World's Columbian Exposition was held in Chicago to mark the 400th anniversary of the discovery of America by Columbus. The first was pre-Columbian architecture as represented by the replica of the Mayan nunnery at Uxmal; the other was Japanese culture. Already aware and intrigued with Oriental art, the latter caught his imagination in the form of a half-scale replica of a wooden temple from the Fujiwara period.

The previous year Wright had gained a degree of recognition with one of his domestic commissions, the Charnley House; furthermore his own house at Oak Park became greatly admired. Now, although he was only a draftsman, clients, many of them wealthy suburban businessmen and Oak Park neighbors, started coming to him personally to design and build their homes. Wright called these his "bootlegged houses." They were done in his own time in evenings and at weekends and holidays and didn't violate his contract with Adler and Sullivan — he was careful to keep to the letter, if not the spirit, of his contract. Such work proved a great financial boon as his five children were proving cripplingly expensive. Inevitably Sullivan found out and, predictably, was not impressed with Wright's explanations. They parted company after a furious row and were not reconciled for twenty years: however, in 1924 Wright wrote Sullivan's definitive obituary.

It was now 1893 and together with several other young architects Frank set up his own practice in Steinway Hall, Chicago. The work flowed in and he was able to build up a successful, if unremarkable, business doing "period" homes for local clients, again many of them his Oak Park neighbors. These comfortably-off men invariably spent more on their houses than they had originally intended — especially if Wright designed the furniture and fittings for the interiors as he liked to do as well — but they were usually ultimately very glad that they had done so!

In 1894, at the age of 27, Wright wrote his first essay on architecture — "The Architect and the Machine" — which he read to the University Guild at Evanston, Illinois. It was the first of many papers and writings in which he would expound his theories. At the same time he completed his first house: for William H. Winslow in River Forest, Illinois. Wright found that he increasingly liked working from home, despite the size of his family. To keep them away from his work, he built himself a separate studio in 1895. There, a couple of years later, he gathered around him a group of enthusiastic young assistants to work under his direction. His most significant works of this period are the Romeo and Juliet Windmill he designed and built for his aunts Nell and Jane Lloyd Jones in Spring Green, Wisconsin, and the 1898 River Forest Golf Club, since demolished.

By 1900 Wright's architectural style had matured and he built the Bradley House and Hickox House in Kankakee, Illinois. He was now into his Prairie House period in which he built 33 houses between roughly 1900 until 1910. Characteristically these were low and spreading houses without attic or basement, emerging from the surrounding landscape and vegetation. Inside the space was open and free, designed around a simple X, L or T shape and filled with light, usually from a ribbon of celestory windows on the first floor under wide-spreading eaves. These popular homes lacked any external ornamentation except lead or art glass windows and an ornamental foliage pattern frieze, often in terra cotta, just below the eaves. Furthermore he brought himself to more than just parochial architectural attention in 1901 when he was commissioned to write two articles in *The Ladies' Home Journal*, "A Home in a Prairie Town" (February, 1901) and "A Small House with 'Lots of Room in It'" (July 1901). His project for the first article was to develop a comfortable home for about $7,000. He accepted the challenge wholeheartedly and

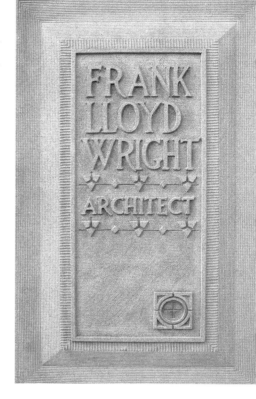

ABOVE: This carved stone appears outside Wright's Oak Park home. His neighbors provided him with many commissions at home and further afield — in Oak Park itself and neighboring River Forest he would build or remodel over 30 structures.

BELOW: The Ward W. Willits House, a splendid example of Wright's Prairie House style. Its living area is dominated by the end wall floor-to-ceiling glazing. Wright designed furniture for the stylish interior.

Frank Lloyd Wright
memorial at Taliesin
East.

he presented a revolutionary approach to flexible, open-plan living. Although nobody took up the idea at the time, it attracted much attention and brought him to a public beyond Illinois and Wisconsin. In time, this innovative concept became to be considered his earliest major contribution to modern architecture and was the germ of his Prairie houses.

Exhausted by the traumas of building the Larkin Company administration headquarters in Buffalo, Frank Lloyd Wright decided to recover with a visit to Japan in 1905, a country whose culture and traditions — particularly artworks — had been of considerable interest to him for some time. Accompanied by his wife and two clients with whom they had struck up a friendship, Mr. and Mrs. Ward W. Willits, Wright took the opportunity to buy a considerable quantity of Japanese art. He was especially attracted by woodblock prints and the work of ukiyo-e artists like Hiroshige, Hokusai, Utamaro, Harunobu, Kiyonaga, and Sharaku. He didn't stop there; he bought bronzes, *kakemono* (Japanese hanging scrolls), ceramics and textiles as well as folding screens of the Monoyama and Edo periods. In time he acquired a valuable collection of Oriental art and became a considerable expert on Japanese works in particular, especially the prints which he so loved.

Three years later this interest in Japanese cultural traditions led him to collaborate with Frederick Gookin, an authority on Japanese prints, to present a collection of Hiroshige prints at Chicago's Institute of Art. They became good friends and Gookin, an enthusiastic fan of all things Japanese, became convinced that Wright was the only man who could design and build the new Imperial Hotel in Tokyo. Gookin, therefore, determined to secure the job for his friend. The existing hotel was about to be pulled down and rebuilt, partly with the intention of attracting more American tourists. One of Gookin's many Japanese contacts was the manager of the Imperial, Aisaku Hayashi, and he eventually convinced him that Wright was the only man who could combine the spirit of Japanese architecture with American building techniques and standards.

However, back in Illinois, Wright had rashly fallen in love with Mamah Borthwick Cheney, the wife of one of his neighborhood clients. Unable to live together in such a conservative society, they decided to flee to Europe, Wright being able to take up a timely offer from the German publisher Ernst Wasmuth to publish a complete monograph of his architectural work to date. So in the fall of 1909 he shut down his Oak Park studio that had thrived for 16 years, and abandoned his wife and six children. At the same time he uncharitably justified his actions by blaming his family for his financial problems, which actually had far more to do with his own extravagance than anything else. Such lame excuses did nothing to reduce the ensuing scandal, which escalated when Mrs. Cheney left her husband and two children to join him in Europe.

Far away from Chicago and the personal reproach, Wright and Mamah settled down to live in Berlin, he to his drawing board and she to a teaching post. For winter they went to Florence to avoid the heavy snow falls, taking a house in Fiesole, near Florence and decided to stay on there, all around them, captivated by the wonderful Tuscan villas and gardens. To help with the vast number of ink drawings required by the monograph, Wright sent for his son Lloyd and one of his draftsmen, Taylor Woolley.

By 1911 the monograph was finished and they decided to return to the United States. But where could they go? Chicago was impossible, so they decided on the old family domains of Spring Green, Wisconsin. Wright's mother helped out by giving him a tract of family land which she had earmarked for a cottage for herself. The land, although very hilly and rocky, was ideal for a rural estate and Wright christened it Taliesin, the Welsh for "shining brow." Wanting to make Mamah his legal wife, Wright pleaded with Catherine for a divorce, but still deeply hurt and angry, she refused.

True, as ever, to his own extravagant impulses, the building of Taliesin proved beyond his means. It turned out to be a never-ending expense and Wright got himself ever deeper into debt. He had intended to open an office in Chicago, but found that he preferred working from his own studio at Taliesin. Here he was able to develop fully and display his ideas of using natural materials and elements combined in a setting of harmony and sympathy with the overall environment. Wooden sculptures were carefully positioned around the house, while bronze, iron, and stone Chinese and Japanese sculpture strayed out into the garden, combining and merging the internal and external worlds. As an integral interior theme, Wright displayed his precious Japanese artifacts: the folding screens were laid flat against the walls bordered by a strip of cypress, while the prints were mounted on soft tan paper and displayed on freestanding easels. Japanese hanging scrolls were hung beside Chinese landscape paintings: all were used as major focal points against the cypress woodwork used throughout the house.

Meanwhile, the German monograph of his work, *Ausgeführte Bauten und Entwürfe von Frank Lloyd Wright,* was published, making his works and name well-known throughout Europe. Commissions were rolling in and he would have made a comfortable living were it not for his penchant for expensive clothes, stylish cars, extravagant living, and, of course, compulsive Japanese art collecting. The commission for the Imperial Hotel in Tokyo was still in the offing and in 1913 Wright returned (with Mamah) to Japan to press his case. By now a number of influential friends and admirers were also calling for him to get the job; even so, Wright still didn't secure the commission until 1914.

He was, however, commissioned by Edward C. Waller to design the Midway Gardens pleasure palace in Chicago. This and other jobs convinced Wright of the necessity of opening a Chicago office to be nearer the majority of his clients and contractors. Then, one day in August 1914 while he was working on the Midway Gardens, he was called home from his Chicago office, back to Taliesin. There a scene of devastation and tragedy was set out before him. A cook had gone berserk; while Mamah and her two visiting children were having lunch, he had locked the doors and poured gasoline around the entrance. He then set fire to the building and, as the victims tried to flee, he attacked them with an axe. Seven bodies were laid out on the lawn in the garden court when Wright arrived

Detail from Wright's poured-concrete master-piece — the Aline Barnsdall House, better known as the Hollyhock House. Monolithic as a Mayan temple, it was built around 1920. The hollyhock theme runs throughout the house, including hollyhock motif dining chairs and carpet. See pages 234–37.

home. As well as Mamah and her children, three apprentices and a work-man were slain, one of them the son of his craftsman, William Weston. Taliesin was a charred ruin. The murderer committed suicide by taking poison, never explaining his motives in the three weeks it took him to die in prison.

Shocked and bereft, Wright nevertheless vowed to rebuild Taliesin — and in the process all but bankrupted himself. Again the building was continually rebuilt and extended into a great rambling building of geo-metrically shaped desert rock pieces superimposed on each other, all with a tent-like canvas roofing — such an innovative composition was only possible in a desert environment. Then out of the blue, from all the letters of sympathy and condolence he received, one letter in particular caught his attention. It was from a woman he had never met, called Miriam Noel. She expressed such empathy through her letter that he agreed to her request to meet him. So started a self-destructive relation-ship that lasted the better part of ten years. Miriam was artistic but unbal-anced, her emotional state aggravated by her addictions. She was also weak and depressed, emotions that Wright felt attracted by, but such raw feelings rapidly took away from their relationship.

In December 1916 they sailed for Tokyo together, where they lived while Wright worked on the Imperial Hotel project for which he had accepted a $300,000 fee. By now Miriam was a social recluse, but given to violent outbursts, many of them rooted in her constant insecurity. Yet somehow they stayed together despite their raging rows. With the money he was earning from the Imperial, Wright bought yet more Japanese art, but also forged ahead with the new Taliesin. To supplement his income further, and as a logical corollary of his own interest, he bought Japanese art for other American collectors, most notably for Mr. and Mrs. William Spalding of Boston, his close friend Frederick Gookin at the Art Institute of Chicago, Howard Masefield of the Metropolitan Museum of Art in New York City, and Sally Casey Thayer whose collection eventually went to the Spencer Museum at the University of Kansas.

Frank Lloyd Wright didn't desert the United States completely during the time he was supervising the building of the Imperial Hotel. He made frequent trips to the midwest and, more particularly, to California. Back in 1914 he had met Aline Barnsdall, heiress to a Pennsylvania oil fortune. She was a keen thespian, whose dream was to build a theatrical com-plex, complete with homes and shops. She was a temperamental woman, prone to extreme mood swings, constantly changing her mind about what she wanted and completely paranoid about being taken advantage of for her money. Despite all the problems and the abandon-ment of the bulk of the project, Wright would complete one of his best known works — the Hollyhock House — and two other houses for her. He maintained that in his entire career no other client had caused him so much trouble, or given him so much grief. The problems were worth overcoming. Recalling the Mayan nunnery replica he'd seen in 1893, the poured concrete structure of the Hollyhock House has since been desig-nated by the American Institute of Architects as one of 17 buildings designed by Wright to be retained as an example of his architectural contribution to American culture.

Wright and Miriam returned full time to the United States in 1922 when the Imperial Hotel was six months away from completion. The project had been all-encompassing, he had designed every aspect of the building down to the carpets and door handles. His ultimate triumph was to produuce an earthquake proof design which survived the 1923 Kanto 'quake which levelled everything else arouund it. At last Catherine agreed to grant him a divorce on the grounds of 12 years' desertion. Wright hoped that by marrying Miriam he would be able to give her the emotional security she so badly needed and this would improve their relationship. Unhappily, this proved a terrible miscalculation: they separated after six intolerable months. Wright returned to Taliesin. On his own now he threw himself into working on a variety of ideas in company with a number of new assistants, many of these eager young architects from Europe. However, no major contracts were coming in.

Wright was convinced that California, particularly southern California, was the place for his future. Its pre-European past gave the landscape an intangible romance, and the fact that much of the state was desert appealed to him — he liked the vastness, the room to spread, and the idea that the land could be literally transformed by the introduction of water. This was nature in the raw, but it could be made accessible. Wright was adamant that it should be experienced by man living in close affinity with the land and the natural elements of nature. To his mind this could only be achieved by the extensive use of the private automobile.

Life took a better turn for Frank Lloyd Wright in November 1924 while visiting his friend, the painter Jerome Blum. One evening they went to the Russian ballet and, while waiting for the performance to start, a striking young woman with long black hair caught up into a bun took the last seat in their box. As luck would have it, Blum had met her at a dinner party in New York not too long before. She was Olgivanna Lazovich Hinzenberg, a dancer from a patrician Montenegrin family who had been educated in Tsarist Russia. She possessed interesting and advanced social ideas, many of them garnered from the Gurdjiff Institute for the Harmonious Development of Man in Fontainebleau, France.

It transpired that they were both waiting for a divorce, and Olgivanna was further fighting for custody of her daughter Svetlana. In fact, her husband pursued her to Chicago to contest the possession of their daughter. Within three months Olgivanna moved into Taliesin and late the following year, she produced Iovanna, a daughter for Wright. Such flagrant immorality put off many potential clients and Wright found work very hard to come by. Meanwhile, at Taliesin, Olgivanna took over the reins of managing the house and servants with the specific intention of removing daily worries and chores from the mind of the great architect, to allow his genius to reside on a higher plain.

Through the 1920s, the majority of Wright's projects were private residences for Californians. Many of these buildings were romantic and dreamlike, reflecting his feelings about living in close harmony with

Detail of the Charles Ennis house, the last of the four "textile-block" houses Wright built in Los Angeles.

The Arizona Biltmore Hotel was probably the largest of Wright's "textile-block" designs. His level of involvement is debated (see page 23) but there are many of his design and ornamentation trademarks all over the building.

nature and the land, and mirroring in the use of decorative stonework, pre-Columbian architecture. In total he saw 24 buildings completed, although a further 30 remained unbuilt, a number of these latter projects cancelled when their patrons lost money in the great stock market crash of 1929.

In spring 1925, disaster visited Taliesin again when an electrical storm started a fire in some faulty wiring. The living quarters were razed to the ground by the conflagration. Rebuilding Taliesin yet again piled up even more debt for Wright at a time when little work was around. His scandalous lifestyle aroused such hostility that, on the advice of close friends, he and Olgivanna quietly withdrew from Wisconsin and moved for the summer of 1926 to a cottage in Minneapolis, where they lived for a time under assumed names. By now Frank Lloyd Wright's career seemed at an end; he was generally considered to be one of the establishment figures in architecture, unable to keep up with contemporary developments in the building world.

With nothing much to occupy him, Wright again took up writing. At the prompting of Olgivanna, he started an autobiography, and began preparing an exhibition of his work that would tour Europe and the United States. Money was still very much a problem and in 1927 he sent a number of his Japanese prints to auction in New York. The sale helped to reduce his debts, but expenses continued to mount and his affairs got so bad that he was forced to turn Taliesin and the remains of his art collections over to the bank. Homeless, he moved to stay in New York with his sister, Maginel Wright Barney, now an illustrator of children's books.

In 1928, the prospect of work at last appeared when he was asked by the McArthur family to act as consultant on the building of the Arizona Biltmore Hotel. While staying for three months in Phoenix, he met Dr. Alexander Chandler, the owner of a large hotel and founder and owner of much of the town of Chandler. He wanted to build a large, elegant, hotel-cum-resort in the desert outside Chandler, where the rich could escape the rigors of winter. The project was called San Marcos-in-the-Desert, and Wright lived on the spot for a time and then at La Jolla in California.

Finally, on August 25, 1928, Frank and Olgivanna married in a quiet ceremony in the garden of an inn in Rancho Santa Fe. Also at much the same time, a number of his friends and former clients formed Frank Lloyd Wright Inc., a scheme to bankroll the great architect and keep him from debt, which also made his return to Taliesin possible.

In the winter of 1929, with his family and followers, Wright returned to the Arizona desert where they built a temporary town out of canvas and box boards. Called Ocotillo Camp, he stayed there while working on the San Marcos project, and liked it so much that the camp became the prototype for the winter home he would design in 1937 for the Taliesin Fellowship — Taliesin West in Scottsdale, Arizona.

The stock market crash of 1929 brought all commissions to an abrupt halt — including, most notably, the San Marcos-in-the-Desert project. The only work he was left with was a large house he was building for his cousin Richard Lloyd Jones, in Tulsa, Oklahoma. Otherwise work was again scarce and Wright had to turn to writing and lecturing for the bulk of his income. In 1931 Wright lectured at New York's New School for Social Research, but he wasn't a very good teacher. His ideas were too individualistic for students to find useful. The following year *An Autobiography* was published by Longmans, Green and Company. Although shamelessly biased and self-promoting, it stimulated new interest in him and his work and young architects started to consider him as the sage but eccentric elder statesman.

With such encouragement and a general revival of interest in his work, Wright established the Taliesin Fellowship at Spring Green. This was conceived along the lines of a utopian community of worker-apprentices who paid a fee to come and work and live with the great architect. The community grew as apprentices arrived, and much of their attitude was fostered by Olgivanna, who put into play her advanced social theories learned at the Gurdjieff Institute. The core of her approach was to deliberately create an almost mystical reverence for Frank Lloyd Wright; he was presented as the revered master at whose feet they were privileged to learn and pay homage. Despite paying for the honor, part of the apprentices' daily routine was to do chores around the house and grounds between working on their assigned design projects. They helped to run the home and office and helped on many of his projects with drawings and model-making. Some of them later went on to work for Wright on Taliesin West. In time his best assistants were given his projects to control and he rarely supervised his work personally (one of the later exceptions to this was the Guggenheim Museum).

The building of Fallingwater in Pennsylvania for Edgar Kaufmanna in 1936, and the completion of the S. C. Johnson & Son Administration Building in Racine, Wisconsin (1936-39) saw Wright's reputation resurge. His confident incorporation of new building methods and materials impressed the new generation of up and coming architects. A major problem of these Depression years was finding good quality, economic houses for middle class families. Wright came up with the concept of the "Usonian" house which would bring into full play new developments in building, in particular the use of pre-cast concrete. (Usonia was Wright's term for the United States and its culture and was first used in his 1925 essay "In the Cause of Architecture: The Third Dimension" published in the Dutch *Wendingen*.) The first Usonian house was built in 1936 for Herbert Jacobs in Madison, Wisconsin and he would build over a hundred more. (See page 212 onward for more about the principles of the Usonian house.) Such homes he foresaw as being integral to his dream of a wide-spreading utopian development he called Broadacre City — a dream project he would work on for the remainder of his life. Wright was also becoming a well-known exponent of decentralization and was very ambivalent towards any form of state control — particularly with regard to building rules and regulations. However he did believe that the government should provide the basic infrastructure. He was not averse to using influence, and to this end he personally — but unsuccessfully —

The entrance lobby of the Johnson's Wax Building.

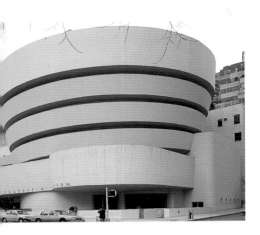

ABOVE: The imposing exterior of the Guggenheim Museum, New York.

BELOW: The sign at Taliesin West, erected in 1953. Wright's final resting place was at Scottsdale. After Olgivanna's death his remains were disinterred and their ashes mingled in a new grave in the Arizona desert.

petitioned the President to protect the Arizona desert from the ravages of the U.S. Army Corps of Engineers who took powerlines right across his panoramic view from Taliesin West.

Between 1940 and 1942, with U.S. involvement in the war in Europe a looming threat, Wright became a vocal opponent of participation. He aired his pacifist views in 10 essays, the most notorious of which was entitled "Wake up America!" (published in *Christian Century* in November 1940). His stance gathered Wright more enemies, as did his sympathy for the Japanese, which he still promoted even after Pearl Harbor. As a consequence he fell out with a number of his friends, including his once close friend Lewis Mumford and even his cousin Richard Lloyd Jones.

In 1943 Duell, Sloan and Pearce published his revised *An Autobiography*, and in June that year a letter came out of the blue from Baroness Rebay asking whether he would consider designing a new museum to contain Solomon R. Guggenheim's collection of non-objective paintings. He was immediately attracted by the prospect, met Guggenheim, and signed a contract with him on June 29, 1943. But the museum had no site for nine months and Wright became increasingly frustrated at not knowing what he had to deal with. This was the inauspicious start of what proved a very enervating period. New York and its bureaucracy, its planning authorities, in particular the Commissioner Robert Moses, became the bane of his life. Intellectually their minds had no meeting point: Moses had plans for New York which included building high-rise, high density housing. Wright, in complete contrast, saw dispersed low-level homes as the only answer to housing the urban masses. A personal antipathy developed, in which Moses did all he could to obstruct the building of the museum.

The battle to build the Guggenheim Museum lasted for the next 16 years, during which time the project consumed Wright. Over such a long period the costs, of course, escalated and accordingly the plans were revised time and again to reduce the expense as much as possible. In total Wright drew up eight complete sets of plans (the first set contained 29 architectural drawings and 13 structural drawings). Guggenheim himself actually believed that building costs would drop in time, so he postponed the project — he was wrong, everything just got more expensive. During the war nothing could be done as all building materials were diverted into the war effort.

For the duration of the Guggenheim project Wright moved to New York, perversely a city that he loved. His favorite place to stay was the Plaza Hotel where he had a two-room apartment refurbished to his specifications. He had always worked where he ate and slept and this was no exception, one room was part office and reception. As usual, he surrounded himself with expensive luxury. He installed sleek black lacquer tables, a golden peach wool carpet and dark purple velvet draperies; for wall coverings he had gold-flecked rice paper and around the room he arranged his oriental art.

In November 1949 Solomon Guggenheim died. The project was in jeopardy for a time until his bequest was sorted out. The following year Harry S. Guggenheim was appointed president of the Foundation and supported Wright in his endeavours to get the building built. Still politically vocal, particularly with his anti-war views, Wright drew the attention of Senator McCarthy from his home state of Wisconsin, who tried to have him impeached as an anti-American communist.

In January 1951 a world touring exhibition of Wright's work entitled "Sixty Years of Living Architecture" opened in Philadelphia. This showed his original drawings, architectural models and huge photographs of many of his buildings and decorative objects. The exhibition arrived in New York in 1953 and helped to keep up the momentum for the Museum. Building work on the Guggenheim finally began in summer 1956, and it opened to the public on October 21, 1959, six months after Wright died. The innovative, spiral building was initially loathed by the public as being totally unsuitable for elegant Fifth Avenue. The artists whose work was displayed inside, hated the way their work was suspended against the sloping, off-white walls.

The entire Guggenheim Museum project was a fight from start to finish and took its toll on Frank Lloyd Wright's health. He returned to Taliesin West to recuperate when the end of the building was in sight. Now aged 91 Wright was operated on in hospital in Phoenix, to remove an intestinal obstruction. Despite his frailty he came through the operation and appeared to be making a good recovery when, five days later on April 9, 1959, he died. His body was taken back to his old home in Spring Green, Wisconsin, where it was placed in the family burial ground a few hundred yards from Taliesin North, next to his mother and Mamah Cheney. There he remained for 26 years until 1985 when Olgivanna died; her last wish was that in death they should be together, so his remains were disinterred and taken to Taliesin West in Arizona, where their ashes were mingled together and buried in a new grave.

When he died, Wright was working on plans for Marin County Civic Center, at San Rafael in California, a complex that included offices, libraries, and spaces for social activities. The project was finished in 1962 after his death. It was the nearest he got to realizing his dream of a utopian city.

By the time of his death, Frank Lloyd Wright was recognized as the greatest architect that America had produced to date. The American Institute of Architects designated 17 of his buildings as deserving of special recognition. These comprise all his personal dwellings — his Home and Studio at Oak Park, Taliesin at Spring Green, and Taliesin West; domestic commissions — the Winslow House, the Kaufmann House ("Fallingwater"), the Hanna "Honeycomb" House, the Robie House, the Ward Willits House, the Aline Barnsdall "Hollyhock" House; — and his public buildings, the Price Tower, the V. C. Morris Gift Shop, the S. C. Johnson (Wax) Building and the Guggenheim Museum; as well three places of worship were listed — the Unitarian Church at Shorewood Hills, the Unity Temple, and the Beth Shalom Synagogue.

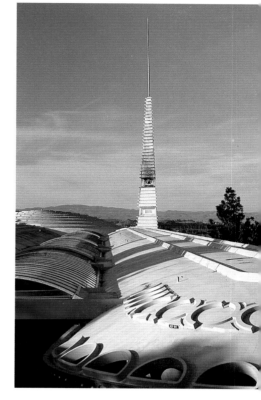

ABOVE: The radio mast atop the Marin County Civic Center's domed library.

BELOW: The Price Company Tower in Bartlesville, Oklahoma.

ALABAMA

The only example of Wright's work in Alabama is in Florence. It is a large Usonian private house built in 1939 and enlarged in 1948. The living area built-in furniture was specially designed by Wright and made from Cypress wood.

STANLEY ROSENBAUM HOUSE (1939)
117 Riverview Drive, Florence, Alabama
Illustrated above and right.
Built for Stanley and Mildred Rosenbaum, this L-plan Usonian house was enlarged in 1948 by Wright himself. It was completely renovated in 1970 with internal modifications and the addition of an outside Japanese garden. See Interior Designs chapter for further pictures and information.
The house is open to the public and guided tours are available by appointment.

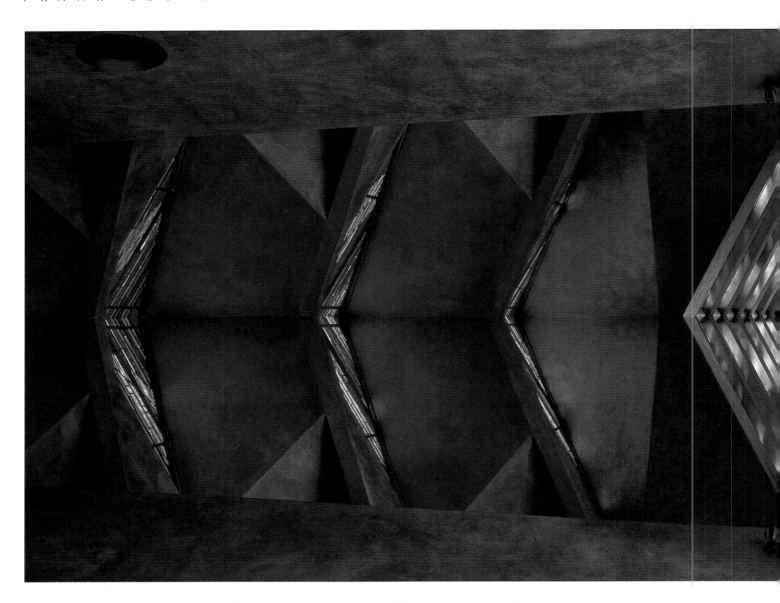

A R I Z O N A

There were 12 examples of Wright's work in Arizona, built between 1927 and 1973, one of which has now been demolished. All that remains of the demolished house, one of five private residences built in Phoenix, is the desert rubblestone wall. The wood terraces and balconies were destroyed by fire in 1942 three years after the house was constructed. However, Arizona is home to Taliesin West, his winter establishment where he died in 1959, making it an important state to visit to take in Wright's life and works.

The first example of Wright's work to be built in Arizona was the Arizona Biltmore Hotel (1927) in Phoenix, the hotel being the largest textile-block design in which he was involved. The state also has the first constructed example of a Usonian "automatic" house. Arthur Pieper, a Taliesin West student, built it himself, making his own blocks. This do-it-yourself approach is the essence of the "automatic" construction.

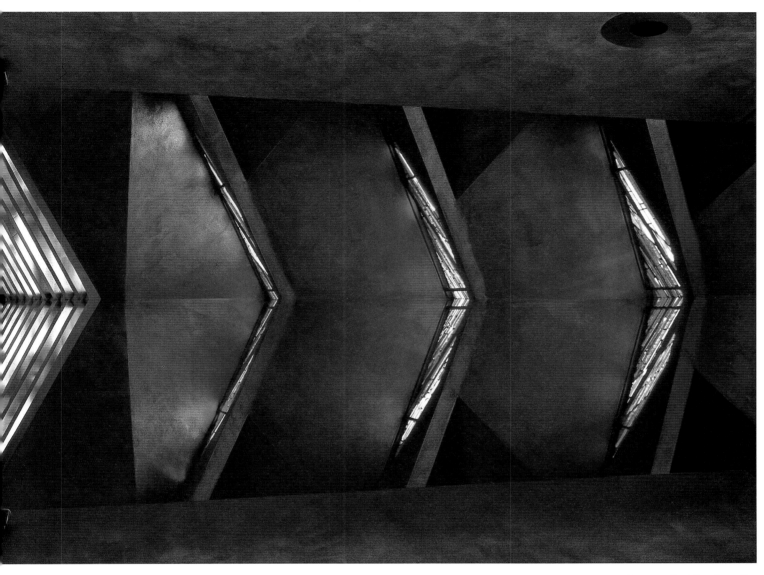

ABOVE and LEFT: Detail and ground view of the First Christian Church, Phoenex. See page 23.

Wright's son David was involved in promoting concrete block construction and his house in Phoenix is constructed of these materials. Because his father's plans were not consistent with concrete construction, a complete re-engineering of the project took place.

Frank Lloyd Wright's winter home for the Taliesin Fellowship, Taliesin West in Scottsdale, offered a new challenge in building materials. The architect conceived the "desert rubblestone wall," which involves large stones set in concrete, to produce a more colorful and natural effect than pure concrete. Taliesin West houses the Taliesin Fellowship for much of the year.

Arizona is notable for being home to both the last residential and the last non-residential designs to be built by Wright. The former is the house he designed for Norman Lykes. Its building was supervised by a member of the Taliesin Fellowship and took place between 1966 and 1968. The last non-residential design was the Gammage Memorial Auditorium of the Arizona State University at Tempe.

Wright's designs are still being built today by the Taliesin Associated Architects (TAA) but the last project to be completed in Arizona was the First Christian Church in Phoenix. Wright first produced plans of a university campus for the Southwest Christian Seminary in 1951. When the university failed to proceed, the First Christian Church decided to go ahead with the chapel, starting work on it in 1971, 12 years after Wright's death in Phoenix.

ARTHUR PIEPER HOUSE (1952)
6442 East Cheney Road, Paradise Valley

This house, built by a Taliesin West student Arthur Pieper, is said to be the first example of a Usonian "automatic" house to be built. It has later additions (a dining room).

HAROLD PRICE Sr HOUSE (1954)
7211 North Tatum, Paradise Valley

Built for Harold Price Sr., who also commissioned the Price Tower in Bartlesville (see Oklahoma and Interior Design sections). The most distinctive feature of the design is the central atrium, its roof raised above concrete pillars, thus serving the dual purpose of allowing in cool air but keeping out rain and direct sun. Its construction is concrete block throughout.

DAVID WRIGHT HOUSE (1950)
5212 East Exeter Road, Phoenix

The home of David, Wright's fourth child, who was the contractor for the house. It is constructed from concrete blocks with a metal roof. The raised living spaces are reached by a spiral ramp, an important feature of many of Wright's designs, for example the V. C. Morris Gift Shop (see California section). Wright also designed the furniture.

ARIZONA BILTMORE HOTEL (1927)
East Sahuaro Drive at Camino Acequia, Phoenix
Illustrated left, below, and right.

The hotel is the largest textile-block design by Wright — although there is some debate about how much of the design was his, as he was called in to act as a consultant by the job architect, Albert McArthur. However, much of the detail work bears his hallmarks, particularly the patterned concrete blocks, the lobby (which is reminiscent of the Imperial Hotel, Wright's demolished Japanese venture), the adjoining single and two-story cottages, and the fabulous multi-colored glass mural adapted from a design in *Liberty* magazine. Guided tours by appointment.

FIRST CHRISTIAN CHURCH (designed 1950)
6750 North 7th Avenue, Phoenix
Illustrated on pages 20 and 21.

Designed by Wright and built after his death. Initial stages of construction were completed 1971–73. The chapel features a stained glass window by a member of the Taliesin Fellowship. Guided tours by appointment.

BENJAMIN ADELMAN HOUSE (1951)
5710 North 30th Street, Phoenix
A two-story building Usonian "automatic" house, the plans for which were conceived before the Pieper House in Paradise Valley but it was built later.

JORGINE BOOMER HOUSE (1953)
5808 North 30th Street, Phoenix
This is a two-story "mountain cottage" constructed from desert rubble-stone.

NORMAN LYKES HOUSE (1959)
6836 North 36th Street, Phoenix
Wright's last residential design to be built, the central living room is of circular plan with all the other parts of the house planned as circular segments. The building is constructed of concrete blocks.

RAYMOND CARLSON HOUSE (1950)
1123 West Palo Verde Drive, Phoenix
This is a three-story building built of wood and cement panels.

GRADY GAMMAGE MEMORIAL AUDITORIUM (1959)
Arizona State University, Apache Boulevard at Mill Avenue, Tempe

Illustrated left, below, and right.

Wright's last non-residential design to be built, it has a circular arcade of 50 tall concrete columns supporting the outer roof. The exterior walls are made of brick and a marble like composition called marblecrete. A pedestrian bridge (illustrated above left) takes the audience from parking lot to auditorium. Guided tours available.

25

TALIESIN WEST (1937–59)
11000 Shea Road, Scottsdale
Illustrated below, right and on pages 28–31, 232–33.

Frank Lloyd Wright's winter home for the Taliesin Fellowship is a complex of buildings which includes a theater, music pavilion, and Sun Cottage. He first started work on the site in 1938 with apprentices from Taliesin North. Every winter for the next twenty-two years, he and his students would continue the work revising and enlarging the complex. It was built using what Wright described as "desert rubblestone" construction. This involved placing large stones at random into forms then pouring concrete around the stones leaving most of the face next to the form exposed. The stone was washed with acid to bring out its coloring. Influenced by the wooden structure erected for the Ocatillo Desert Camp, Wright built much of Taliesin West from linen canvas on redwood frames, which diffused the harsh desert sun; today fibreglass and steel have replaced much of this. Taliesin West has been designated by the AIA as one of 17 examples of Wright's architectural contribution to American culture that must be kept unspoiled. It is open to the public and tours are available.

ABOVE, RIGHT, and FAR
RIGHT: More scenes of
Taliesin West.

TALIESIN WEST.

ABOVE and FAR RIGHT:
The interiors of Taliesin
West were well appoint-
ed, with carefully
designed work and
leisure areas.

CALIFORNIA

Buildings from Wright's designs in California span almost ninety years from the first in Montecito (196 Hot Springs Road) to "Eaglefeather" in Malibu (32436 West Mulholland Highway), set high in the Santa Monica Mountains. The first of his California houses, the Stewart House of 1909 — a lovely drawing of which appeared in the 1910 Wasmuth portfolio of his work (see Introduction) — was a Midwestern Prairie house on the Pacific Coast. It would not have looked out of place on the shores of Lake Michigan. There could not be a greater contrast between the Stewart House and his next two Californian projects, which were heavily influenced in appearance by the pre-Columbian temples of the Maya and in layout by the Italian villas he and Mamah Cheney had visited while in Florence in 1910–11. The Hollyhock House is undoubtedly one of his great masterpieces, intended to be part of a larger complex of buildings only two of which (and a pergola and children's pool) were

ABOVE and LEFT: The Hanna House is also known as the "Honeycomb House" because it is designed on a hexagonal system as is a beehive.

subsequently built. It has been a public park since 1927 when owner Aline Barnsdall gave it to the City of Los Angeles. It was followed by the first of his four textured-concrete "textile-block" houses: "La Miniatura" (645 Prospect Crescent, Pasadena), for Alice Millard. All four of the "textile-block" houses (the others are the Charles Ennis, John Storer, and Samuel Freeman houses) involved the use of precast concrete blocks, decorated on both sides, which were bound together at the building site with steel tie rods and poured concrete. These perforated blocks could be used to allow light into the house sometimes inset with glass. All the houses, as was usual with Wright, were carefully landscaped under the supervision of his eldest son, Lloyd Wright, who was also involved in on-site contracting.

Wright maintained an office in Los Angeles and it is therefore not surprising that, apart from the states on the shores of the Great Lakes, there are more examples of Wright's works in California than anywhere else in the country. However, despite this, following his 1920s work in California, he had to wait until 1936 before receiving another commission in the state. By this time he had devised the first Usonian house (the Herbert Jacobs House, see page 188) and his next work in California, all around San Fransisco, reflects this. The 1936 Honeycombe House for Paul R. Hanna, the Sidney Bazett House (1938–40), and the George D. Sturges House (1939) are all of masonry and redwood, the first two designed around hexagonal modules — thus the "Honeycomb" of the Hanna House. The Bazett House is Usonian in its use of space, with the kitchen/workspace at the center of the design; the Sturges House is dramatically cantilevered out of the hillside. Many subsequent residential buildings in California — those, for example, for Mrs. Clinton Walker, Maynard P. Buehler, or Robert Berger — are similarly Usonian, although the use of "rubblestone" is apparent in the buildings for Arch Oboler and Robert Berger, and the return to concrete blocks is managed interestingly in the Randall Fawcett, Robert G. Walton, and George Ablin houses.

Wright's commercial and civic buildings in California are also impressive and important. There's the V. C. Morris Gift Shop of 1949, with its brick facade, Romanesque splayed portal arch, and circular ramp, the latter a Guggenheim in microcosm. In 1952, in a fashionable downtown section of Beverly Hills (332 North Rodeo Drive), the Anderton Court Shops were also built around a ramp — and a distinctive mast. Mast was also the a dramatic exclamation point in the design of the futuristic Marin County Civic Center in San Rafael, Wright's only work for the US Government. The design and construction of this complex was underway when Wright died in 1959 and it was finished under the aegis of Aaron Green, William Wesley Peters, and the Taliesin Associated Architects. It gives us a vision of what Wright's dream city —Broadacre City — could have been, and also exemplifies how innovative and forward looking Wright's architectural designs were even in his nineties. This, and the earlier unbuilt Huntington Hartford project of 1947, could be from the set of a science fiction movie!

THIS PAGE and OPPO-
SITE: The George Ablin
House (see page 36).

ARTHUR C. MATHEWS HOUSE (1950)
83 Wisteria Way, Atherton
A brick-built house with two parallel wings emanating from a central dining area segment, thus producing an enclosed terrace and garden area.

GEORGE ABLIN HOUSE (1958)
4260 Country Club Drive, Bakersfield
Illustrated pages 34–35.
The contrast between the large south facing living room of glass and wood and the pool-side main construction of salmon concrete block — some perforated to provide windows — is very striking.

HILARY & JOE FELDMAN HOUSE (Designed in 1939, built in 1974)
13 Mosswood Road, Berkeley
Built long after Wright's death, this Usonian house required 30,000 bricks. California clearheart redwood is used in the trim and for the board and batten walls. The original design was for the Lewis N. Bell House, intended for a west Los Angeles placement.

ANDERTON COURT SHOPS (1952)
332 North Rodeo Drive, Beverly Hills
Illustrated above and right.

This group of shops on four levels in a desirable Beverley Hills location is accessed by means of an upward winding ramp. The key visual element is the striking mast around which the ramp is built. Still open to the public.

WILBUR C. PEARCE HOUSE (1950)
5 Bradbury Hills Road, Bradbury
A Usonian house designed — like the second Herbert Jacobs House and the Laurent House designed in 1949 — in circular segments with a long curving living room, a bank of Wright's hallmark seats, and a promenade terrace in front.

GEORGE D. STURGES HOUSE (1939)
449 Skyeway Drive, Brentwood Heights
Illustrated on pages 48–49.
Alarmingly cantilevered out from a hillside, this house is constructed from brick and wood siding. The whole east side of the house opens out onto a balcony.

RIGHT: The Charles Ennis House. See page 42.

Mrs CLINTON WALKER HOUSE (1948)
Scenic Road at Martin Street, Carmel
Illustrated above left.
A Usonian stone house rising from a rocky promontory on the beach front, looking out over Monterey Bay. The metal living room roof is cantilevered away from the masonry core so that no weight rests on the corbelling bands of glass. Landscape architect was Thomas D. Church.

SIDNEY BAZETT HOUSE (1938-40)
101 Reservoir Road, Hillsborough
Illustrated on pages 50–51.
Wright's second house in San Francisco is of brick and redwood batten, designed in hexagons, with a Usonian workspace.

JOHN STORER HOUSE (1923)
8161 Hollywood Boulevard, Hollywood
Illustrated below left.
The second of the "textile-block" houses, this features a two-story living room with wings to each side (bedrooms west, service east). Construction was supervised by Lloyd Wright who also landscaped the site.

SAMUEL FREEMAN HOUSE (1923)
1962 Glencoe Way, Hollywood
The last and smallest of the "textile-block" houses built in the foothills of the Santa Monica Mountains. Supervision of the construction and landscaping were by Lloyd Wright. Open to the public. Tours available.

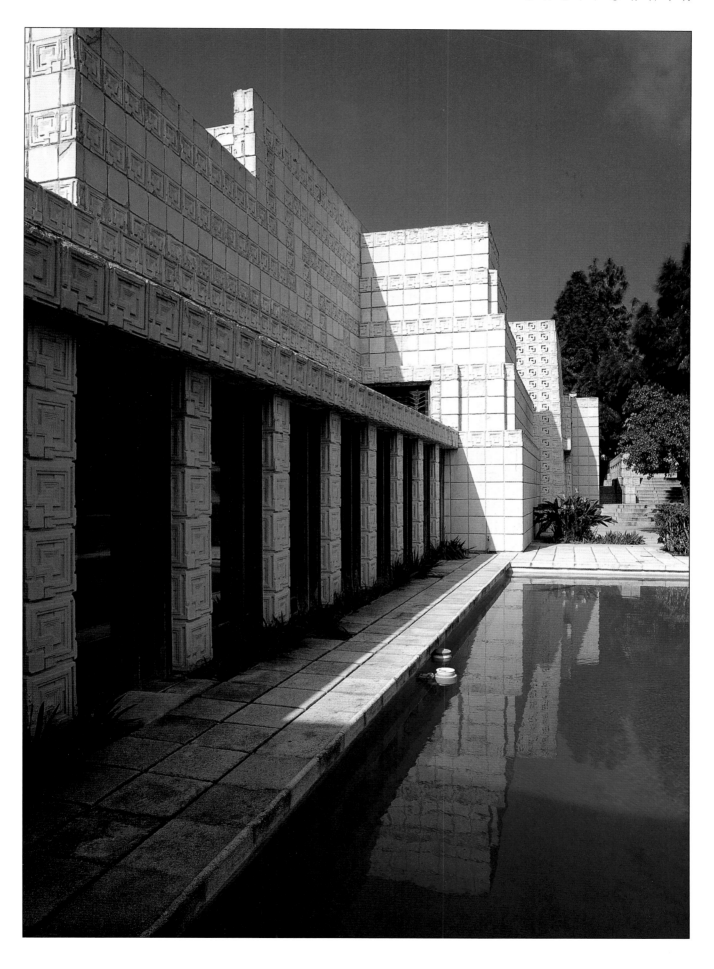

LEFT and OPPOSITE:
The Charles Ennis
House.
See page 42.

CHARLES ENNIS HOUSE (1923)
2655 Glendower Avenue, Los Angeles
Illustrated on pages 39, 40, and 41.
The third and largest of the four Los Angeles "textile-block" houses is even more massively Mayan than the others. It has a pyramidic feel to it. Lloyd Wright supervised construction. Guided tours available.

ALINE BARNSDALL HOUSE — THE HOLLYHOCK HOUSE (1917)
4808 Hollywood Boulevard, Los Angeles
Illustrated on pages 54–59.
One of three Californian buildings listed by the A.I.A., the Hollyhock House also suggests a Mayan Temple. The house is centered on a living room which leads out into an enclosed garden court and pool. Open to the public. Tours available. See also Interior Designs section.

RANDALL FAWCETT HOUSE (1955)
21200 Center Avenue, Los Banos
This two-winged house is constructed from battered concrete block. The wings make 60 degree angles to the main living space which contains a walk-in fireplace.

ARCH OBOLER GATEHOUSE AND RETREAT (1940-46)
32436 West Mulholland Highway, Malibu
Illustrated below right.
This desert rubblestone wall construction, with additions designed in 1944 and 1946 by Wright, was never completed. Horizontal wood siding is used in addition to the rubblestone.

ROBERT G. WALTON HOUSE (1957)
417 Hogue Road, Modesto
A T-plan Usonian concrete block house with wood fascia and trim

GEORGE C. STEWART HOUSE (1909)
196 Hot Springs Road, Montecito
Illustrated above left and above right.
The first of Wright's California houses, its design was completed shortly before Wright left for Europe. A Prairie house, covered with redwood board, it has two stories.

MAYNARD P. BUEHLER HOUSE (1948)
6 Great Oak Circle, Orinda
An L-plan concrete-block and wood house. The sleeping quarters are in the long leg of the L with the work space in the short leg.

ALICE MILLARD HOUSE (1923)
645 Prospect Crescent, Pasadena
Illustrated left.

The first of Wright's four "textile-block" houses this — for Mrs. George Madison — has become known as "La Miniatura." It was constructed by stacking concrete blocks adjacent to and on top of each other without visible mortar joints. The supervision of the construction of the house, with its two-story high living room, was undertaken by Lloyd Wright.

BELOW: Signature tile from the Robert Berger House.

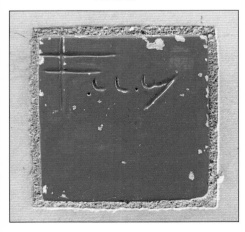

PILGRIM CONGREGATIONAL CHURCH (1958)
2850 Foothill Boulevard, Redding
Illustrated on pages 52–53.
This is only part of a much wider scheme which was never finished after Wright's death. Desert rubblestone wall construction is set against a main roof suspended by white concrete pylons. Open to the public.

ROBERT BERGER HOUSE (1950)
259 Redwood Road, San Anselmo
Illustrated above.
A Usonian house of one story constructed from rubblestone and wood. Set into the steep slopes of the hillside, it was built by Berger himself.

V. C. MORRIS GIFT SHOP (1948)
140 Maiden Lane, San Francisco

One of the seventeen buildings designated to be retained by the A.I.A. Circular forms are employed inside and behind the brick facade of this building which boasts a circular ramp from entrance to lower sales area. Originally a gift shop, it has been renovated and variously used as a dress shop and art gallery. Open to the public.

KARL KUNDERT MEDICAL CLINIC (1955)
1106 Pacific Street, San Luis Obispo

Pierced wood panels with glass inset (like those used on the 1955 Randall Fawcett House) make up the clerestory, to admit patterned light. Wright wanted to build in "textile-blocks" but planning laws stopped this.

MARIN COUNTY CIVIC CENTER (1957)
North San Pedro Road at U.S. 101, San Rafael
Illustrated above, right, and overleaf.

Wright's sole works for the U.S. Government. The Post Office is a

ABOVE AND BELOW:
Marin County Hall of
Justice.

45

nearly circular structure of concrete block and forms. The Hall of Justice and the Administration building are of concrete blocks. The pylon was intended to be a radio tower. Open to the public.

PAUL R. & JEAN S. HANNA HOUSE (1936)
737 Frenchman's Road, Stanford

One of the seventeen buildings designated to be retained by the A.I.A., the "Honeycombe House" is now maintained by Stanford University. Brick-built externally, many of the internal walls are wood and were designed to be moveable — especially to change the layout of the play-room as the owners' children grew up. The Usonian building originally had a copper roof (since replaced); it was Wright's first in the Bay area.

THIS PAGE and
OPPOSITE: The Sturges
House, see page 38.

ABOVE, LEFT and FAR LEFT: The Bazett House, see page 38.

ABOVE, RIGHT and FAR
RIGHT: The Pilgrim
Congressional Church,
see page 44.

ABOVE, RIGHT and
OPPOSITE PAGE: The
Hollyhock House, see
page 42.

PREVIOUS PAGE,
ABOVE, RIGHT and FAR
RIGHT: The Hollyhock
House, see page 42.

CONNECTICUT

RIGHT: The Library of the Florida Southern College at Lakeland. See page 64.

There are only two examples of Wright's work in Connecticut, both private residences built in the 1950s. The house in New Canaan is the more interesting of the two. Called "Tivanna", after an Australian aboriginal word for "running water," it is built in the hills beside a pond of the Noroton river. The pond has been dammed to create a waterfall and a series of fish-steps built to facilitate the passage of fish through the extensive grounds of the house, which also contain an extraordinary variety of flora. Within the grounds there is a treehouse designed by William Wesley Peters, Taliesin Architects' chief architect. The free standing furniture of the house is of Wright's original design.

JOHN L. RAYWARD HOUSE (1955)
432 Frog Town Road, New Canaan

"Tirvanna" is a solar lenin cycle with an extension added by second owner Herman R. Shepherd. Concrete block construction combines with Philippine mahogany and glass. The swimming pool separates the living room from its 18-foot drop to the pond.

FRANK S. SANDER HOUSE (1952)
121 Woodchuck Road, Stamford

A brick foundation and core house, complemented by wood siding, which juts out from a rocky promontory, "Springbough" was restored and freshly landscaped in the 1990s. It is noted for its cantilevered living room.

DELAWARE

The only example of Wright's work in Delaware was built in 1956.

DUDLEY SPENCER HOUSE (1956)
619 Shipley Road, Wilmington

Single-story stone-built house with a hemicycle-plan living room facade opening out onto a terrace.

WM. M. HOLLIS
EXHIBITION AND SEMINAR ROOM

F L O R I D A

Florida does not boast a large quantity of Frank Lloyd Wright buildings, but what it does have is the campus of the Florida Southern College, Lakeland. It gives us a chance to see how Wright planned and executed buidings on a grand scale — although not so grand a scale as the projected Broadacre City. Offered the job by president of the college Dr. Ludd Spivey, Wright's plan for the campus was conceived in 1938 with the buildings being completed 1938–53. The most remarkable of the buildings, and certainly the tallest (the plan kept a uniformly low height on the other structures), was the Annie Pfeiffer Chapel, whose decorative steel tower stands out from everywhere else on the campus. It was designed as a means of lighting the interior of the chapel and works brilliantly. Wright's only other work in Florida is a private house in Tallahassee

LACY DAY EDGE JR

WM J DAVIS

JOE P ELLIS

THE FLORIDA SOUTH-ERN COLLEGE. See page 64.

ABOVE: The Industrial Arts Building.

LEFT: Planetarium and Science and Cosmography Building.

FLORIDA SOUTHERN COLLEGE (1938–53)
South Johnson Avenue at Lake Hollingworth Drive, Lakeland
Illustrated on pages 61–67.

Wright's buildings at the university are the Pfeiffer Chapel (1938), three Seminar Buildings (1940), the Library (1941), the Industrial Arts Building (1942), the Administration Building (1945), the Science and Cosmography Building (1953), and the Minor Chapel (1954). Esplanades — necessary to shelter students from on the one hand tropical downpours and the other a fierce summer sun — were built in 1946 to link all Wright's buidings on the campus; those buildings not linked were built by other architects. In the case of the Industrial Arts and the Science and Cosmography buildings, the esplanades form an extension of their outer walls; elsewhere they run between the other structures. The buildings were made from "textile-block" textured concrete — often inset with colored glass — brick and steel. Much of the hard construction work, the pouring of the concrete for the textured blocks and floor slabs, was done by the college students and set against their college costs. The site is open to the public.

THE FLORIDA SOUTH-
ERN COLLEGE:

ABOVE LEFT: The Annie
Pfeiffer Chapel.

BELOW LEFT: The minor
Chapel.

ABOVE: Esplanade.

LEFT: Industrial Arts
Building.

RIGHT and BELOW:
THE FLORIDA
SOUTHERN COLLEGE.
See page 64.

RIGHT: Detail of
Administrative Building

BELOW: Interior.

GEORGE LEWIS HOUSE (1952)
3117 Okeeheepkee Road, Tallahassee

This two-story residence is Wright's only private house built in Florida. The lower story of the hemicycle building is of concrete block with the upper being wood-sheathed.

IDAHO

Wright's only work in Idaho is a private residence in Bliss, a one-room house built high on the bluffs above the banks of the Snake River.

ARCHIE BOYD TEATER STUDIO (1952)
Old Hagerman Highway, Bliss
Built from a paralleogram module this spacious studio residence has plate glass opening it to the sunlight. Its construction is of quarzite stone and oak and it has a concrete slab floor. It was substantially renovated in the 1980s.

INDIANA

Wright's home in Indiana, only five houses, spans five decades. The earliest, a Prairie House in South Bend is best known for its living room – as is the 1948 Henry Mosslery House. The strangest is the "teepee"-like structure of the Richard Davis House which derived from a 1920s project.

RICHARD DAVIS HOUSE (1950)
1119 Overlook Road, Marion
This remarkable design is constructed from painted concrete block and is cedar shingled with redwood trim. It works like an octagonal "teepee" and the living room rises to the full height of some 38 feet.

ANDREW F. H. ARMSTRONG HOUSE (1939)
Cedar Trail at The Ledge, Ogden Dunes
Cleverly fitted to the contours of the site, this house has been restored following some years of neglect, with additions by John H. Howe, which includes a garage.

HERMAN T. MOSSBERG HOUSE (1948)
1404 Ridgedale Road, South Bend
A two-story L-plan house. It is constructed of red brick and cypress with cedar shingles. The L-wing contains sleeping quarters on the second floor whilst the living room forms the largest segment of the plan. It is built on a corner lot and the L encloses a patio.

K. C. DeRHODES HOUSE (1906)
715 West Washington Street, South Bend

The side entrances of this building turn a simple rectangle into a cruciform plan. It is a Prairie style house typically wood-trimmed and plaster-surfaced. With a substantial living room making the height of the building. It was a club for some years but has been restored.

JOHN E. CHRISTIAN HOUSE (1954)
1301 Woodland Avenue, West Lafayette
A four-foot-square module structure. This single story house with a clerestory is built from brick and wood. The clerestory has a copper fascia.

BELOW: Dr William H. Copeland House..

ILLINOIS

Wright moved to Chicago in 1887, at age twenty, when he went to work as a draftsman at Adler & Sullivan. Illinois was where Wright spent most of his working life and consequently the state in general — and, of course, Chicago and Oak Park in particular — has more examples of his work than any other and many of his most important, and beautiful, designs. Today, the starting point of any examination of the works of Frank Lloyd Wright is in the first extant house of his career: his own house and studio in Oak Park (see pages 94 and 95 for illustrations), built 1889–1909, is one of seventeen of Wright's buildings designated by the A.I.A. to be preserved as examples of his architectural contribution to American culture. (In fact, Wright's son, John Lloyd, claims that the original design for the Abraham Lincoln Center (see page 76) was his father's first architectural work.) The house has been restored to the state it was

LEFT: Bust of FLW outside Austin Gardens, Oak Park.

TOP LEFT: The Harem. See the Frank Wright Thomas House on page 86.

ABOVE: Hen coup in the Fabyan grounds.

ABOVE and BELOW RIGHT: The Fabyan House at 1511 Batavia Road. See page 80.

BELOW: The Kissam House. See page 80.

in before Wright left in 1909. As there was no other client involved, until he left for Taliesin in 1911 Wright used 951 Chicago Avenue as an area of experimentation, remodeling the original six-room, shingled house.

Wright gained all his early experience at Adler & Sullivan and rose rapidly within the firm until he was given a five-year contract in 1889. He assumed responsibility for all Adler & Sullivan's residential commissions from 1890. An example of this period is the Charnley House (see pages 78, 104 and 105).

While still at Adler & Sullivan, Wright's growing reputation led him to being approached to design houses independently. To meet the mounting costs of a young family, and for the experience and control working outside the company would give him, Wright produced several "bootlegged" houses. Examples include the Walter H. Gale House (see page 85), the Blossom House (see page 76), and the Emmond House (see page 84). While he played fair and designed them outside working hours, when Sullivan discovered that he was moonlighting the quarrel led to his departure from the firm.

He set up his own office in Chicago and his first independent commission after leaving Adler & Sullivan was the William H. Winslow House (see page 89) in River Forest, another of Wright's buildings to be listed by the A.I.A. In fact, including this and his home and studio there are five listed Wright houses in Illinois, the others being the first Prairie house, which was built for Ward W. Willits (see page 82), the Unity Temple — the first significant American piece of architecture to use poured concrete (see page 87) — and the Robie House (see page 79), which is considered to be Wright's best example of Prairie masonry with its precise Roman brickwork.

At the turn of the century Wright's work began to move in the direction of his Prairie style houses. These houses had low, sweeping rooflines hanging over uninterrupted walls of windows; his plans were centered on massive brick or stone fireplaces at the heart of the house; his rooms became increasingly open to one another; and the overall configuration of his plans became more and more asymmetrical, reaching out toward some real or imagined prairie horizon. The first Prairie Houses were those built for Harley Bradley and his brother-in-law Warren Hickox in Kankakee, Illinois. At this time Wright was working with Webster Tomlinson, the only partner he ever had, and one of their collaborations was the first of Wright's Prairie style houses to be built in Oak Park (the Frank Wright Thomas House at 210 Forest Avenue, which was dubbed the "Harem"). Other collaborations at this time included the Davenport House (see page 89) — important because it is a clearly executed example of the second of Wright's plans for *The Ladies' Home Journal* and the article "A Small House with 'Lots of Rooms in It',"and the Fricke House (see page 85).

Wright was not just designing houses in this period: he was looking at every detail of the interiors as well. In collaboration with artists like George Niedecken (murals in the Dana-Thomas House) and Richard

Bock (sculptures in the Heller and Dana-Thomas Houses) he was producing all the designs for the interior content, too — furniture, fittings, carpets, lights — everything

There's no doubt that the best way to see the work of Frank Lloyd Wright's early years is to visit the side-by-side suburban developments of Oak Park and River Forest on the west of Chicago. There are thirty of his structures there — residential property, the Unity Temple, and his own home. It would be work in Oak Park that would lead to Wright's change of life in 1909 and end the first, Illinois-based, period of his long career. For it was at 520 North East Avenue, Oak Park, in 1903 that Wright designed a property for Edwin H. Cheney and his wife Mamah Borthwick Cheney. Following a long affair with Mamah, Wright scandalized his friends, clients, and Chicago society by leaving his wife and six children — and the thriving architectural practice he had built up — for Europe. His return would see him setting up in Spring Green, Wisconsin.

Wright would build other buildings in Illinois — 1915 saw the Ravine Bluffs Development at Glencoe. This was a housing development, including six houses, concrete sculptures and a bridge marking the entrance to the development. The last of Wright's designs to be constructed in Illinois is the house in Barrington Hills (1265 Donlea Road) built in 1956: it is one of the four prefabricated house designs by Wright for the Marshall Erdman Company.

WILLIAM B. GREENE HOUSE (1912)
1300 Garfield Avenue, Aurora
Illustrated above left.
The plaster surface, wood trim and hipped roof are all common elements of Wright's work in Illinois. The house was extended in 1926 and an enclosed porch was added in 1961.

ALLEN FRIEDMAN HOUSE (1956)
200 Thornapple, Bannockburn
A Y-plan house, the intersection of the Y houses the kitchen and entry area; the wings containing sleeping quarters, living room and carport.

LOUIS B. FREDRICK HOUSE (1954)
County Line Road, Barrington Hills
This three-bedroom house is built from buckskin range brick and Philippine mahogany.

CARL POST HOUSE (1956)
265 Donlea Road, Barrington Hills
One of the four prefabricated house designs by Wright for the Marshall Erdman Company. This L-plan house has the kitchen and dining facilities in the short leg with the living room below the entrance at the inner intersection of the L. The house has a masonry core and is built of brick with horizontal board and batten siding on the bedroom wing.

A. W. GRIDLEY HOUSE (1906)
605 North Batavia Avenue, Batavia
Illustrated right and below.

A Prairie style house of cruciform plan on the ground floor with a T-plan at the second story. It has a plastered surface with stained wood trim and the large open porch has no upper level.

W. H. PETTIT MEMORIAL CHAPEL (1906)
Harrison at Webster, Belvidere
Illustrated on pages 98 and 99.

The chapel adjoining the cemetery (which is open to the public) is a T-plan, plaster-surfaced, wooden, one-story building.

JAMES CHARNLEY HOUSE (1891)
1365 North Astor Street, Chicago
Illustrated on pages 108 and 109.

The style and simplicity of this house was ahead of its time. It was originally built symetrically about an east-west axis. Later additions squared off the dining room bay window. Tours by appointment only.

ROBERT W. ROLOSON APARTMENTS (1894)
3213-3219 Calumet, Chicago

This was the first of Wright's "apartment" projects and is the only built example of city row houses. The brown brick row is noted for its abstract stone work.

GEORGE BLOSSOM GARAGE (1907)
1322 East 49th Street, Chicago
This Prairie style garage of Roman brick with wood trim is built on the back of Wright's Colonial Revival style house.

ABRAHAM LINCOLN CENTER (1903)
700 East Oakwood Boulevard, Chicago
Illustrated left.
Wright's son John Lloyd claims the original design for this building was his father's first architectural work and should be dated 1888. Originally intended as a community center when the Reverend Jenkin Lloyd Jones commissioned it, the building was finally built in a changed form in 1903 under the auspices of Dwight Heald Perkins.

S. A. FOSTER HOUSE (1900)
12147 Harvard Avenue, Chicago
The Oriental influence is evident in the curved, upward rising roof lines although Wright, at this time, had not yet visited Japan. Private residence and stable.

WARREN McARTHUR HOUSE AND STABLE (1892)
4852 Kenwood Avenue, Chicago
In the house Roman brick was used up to the window sill and plastered above. The house and stable were both remodeled in 1900. Warren McArthur's son Albert was the project architect on the Arizona Biltmore Hotel.

GEORGE BLOSSOM HOUSE (1892)
4858 Kenwood Avenue, Chicago
Illustrated page 106.
This house with its clapboard siding is a classic example of Colonial Revival architecture. It is built on a symmetrical plan and contrasts sharply with the Prairie style garage built at a later date (1907) on the back (1322 East 49th Street, above).

ROBERT W. EVANS HOUSE (1908)
9914 Longwood Drive, Chicago
A Prairie structure built from a basic square extended into a cruciform plan. The house exists pretty much in its original form apart from the addition of a stone veneer.

J. J. WALSER HOUSE (1903)
42 North Central Avenue, Chicago
A typical Prairie style house built of wood with plaster surface.

EMIL BACH HOUSE (1915)
7415 Sheridan Road, Chicago

Illustrated left
A cantilever design is employed here to enable the second story of the house to overhang the first. Apart from the fact that the wood and plaster has been painted, the house is unaltered with its original brick-work.

ROOKERY BUILDING OFFICE ENTRANCE AND LOBBY (1905)
209 South LaSalle Street, Chicago
The only work that Wright did in this skyscraper was the remodeling of the entrance and lobby. This has been carefully restored over the last few years and is worth seeing if you are passing.

JESSIE M. ADAMS HOUSE (1900)
9326 South Pleasant Avenue, Chicago
Illustrated above
This house is untypical of Wright's designs with its double-hung windows. Jessie Adams's husband William was contracted for the Husser and Heller houses.

E-Z POLISH FACTORY AND OFFICES (1905)
3005-3017 West Carroll Avenue, Chicago
Illustrated above left.

Commissioned by the brothers Darwin D. and W. E. Martin, the upper floors of this building were rebuilt after a fire in 1913. Most of the windows have now been bricked in although a painted mural still survives on the main office floor.

WALLER APARTMENTS (1895)
2840–2858 West Walnut Street, Chicago
Illustrated below right.

Five blocks of apartments. One has already been destroyed by fire; the others are due to be restored.

ISIDORE HELLER HOUSE (1896)
5132 Woodlawn Avenue, Chicago
Illustrated above and left.

An I-plan of rectangular interlocking spaces. The exterior of the house is

of Roman brick and the third story is decorated with figures by Bock.

FREDERICK C. ROBIE HOUSE (1906)
5757 Woodlawn Avenue, Chicago
Illustrated above.
Open to the public, with regular guided tours, this house has been designated a National Landmark as Wright's best example of the Prairie masonry structure.

ROBERT MUELLER HOUSE (1909)
1 Millikin Place, Decatur
The basic design of this house belong to Wright; the interior treatment of the living and dining spaces were the work of Von Holst and Mahony.

E. P. IRVING HOUSE (1909)
2 Millikin Place, Decatur
This house, as 1 Millikin Place, had as many as three designers. It has been suggested that the house is too tall to be a true Wright design.

FRANK L. SMITH BANK (1905)
122 West Main Street, Dwight
Illustrated far right, center.
First National Bank. This building with its cut-stone exterior was renovated in 1970 and is open to the public during banking hours.

F. B. HENDERSON HOUSE (1901)
301 South Kenilworth Avenue, Elmhurst
This is a T-plan building, its hipped roof suggesting a Prairie house. The plan was a collaboration with Webster Tomlinson.

CHARLES E. BROWN HOUSE (1905)
2420 Harrison Street, Evanston
Illustrated above left.
With a rectangular plan and an open front porch, this house is built with horizontal board and batten with plaster under the eaves and between the top-story windows. The double-hung windows are a rarity in Wright designs (see 9326 South Pleasant Avenue, Chicago).

FREDERICK NICHOLS HOUSE (1906)
1136 Brassie Avenue, Flossmoor
This is a cube design built with stained lapped wood. Often referred to as the "Nicholas" House because of a Wrightian misspelling.

COL. GEORGE FABYAN HOUSE (1907)
1511 Batvia Road, Geneva
Illustrated on page 73.
Wright did remodeling work to this house on Col. Fabyan's game preserve, chiefly to the living room, some of the second story and various exterior details. Now a museum, it is open in the summer months.

D. P. HOYT HOUSE (1906)
318 South Fifth, Geneva
Illustrated below left and bottom right.
This is a Prairie style house built to a square-plan with a plastered surface and stained wood trim.

LUTE F. KISSAM HOUSE (1915)
1023 Meadow Road, Glencoe
Illustrated on page 72.
Located in the Ravine Bluffs Development [see Sylvan Road, Glencoe]. The main square of the house has an open porch attached.

WILLIAM F. ROSS HOUSE (1915)
1027 Meadow Road, Glencoe
Located in the Ravine Bluffs Development [see Sylvan Road, Glencoe]. The house is in its original form with an added porch (not by Wright).

HOLLIS R. ROOT HOUSE (1915)
1030 Meadow Road, Glencoe
Located in the Ravine Bluffs Development [see Sylvan Road, Glencoe]. Very similar to the Perry House, the Root House was badly neglected until restored sympathetically in the 1980s.

WILLIAM F. KIER HOUSE (1915)
1031 Meadow Road, Glencoe
Illustrated center left.
Located in the Ravine Bluffs Development [see Sylvan Road, Glencoe]. This square-plan house has a hipped roof and its porch has been modified.

E. D. BRIGHAM HOUSE (1915)
790 Sheridan Road, Glencoe
The only 1915 house in Glencoe that Wright designed independent of Booth's concern (see page 82) its design dates back to 1908. The house was restored in the 1980s although the garage, built at the same time, was demolished in 1968.

W. A. GLASNER HOUSE (1905)
850 Sheridan Road, Glencoe
Illustrated above right.
This house features organization of space similar to later Usonian designs in that no separate room was planned for dining. The rough sawn finish on the wood is typical of the many Prairie style houses with their horizontal board and batten exteriors. The house was renovated in 1926 and again in 1938 with restoration in 1972-1973.

SHERMAN M. BOOTH HOUSE (1915)
265 Sylvan Road, Glencoe
Illustrated above.
Located in the Ravine Bluffs Development [see page 82].
This house belonged to Sherman M. Booth, Wright's lawyer, who commissioned the Ravine Bluff's Development.

CHARLES R. PERRY HOUSE (1915)
272 Sylvan Road, Glencoe
Located in the Ravine Bluffs Development [see next entry]. Square plan three-bedroom plaster and wood house.

RAVINE BLUFFS DEVELOPMENT (1915)
Sylvan Road, Glencoe
Illustrated top and bottom left.
A housing development of six houses commissioned by Sherman M. Booth. In addition to the houses there are poured concrete sculptures and a bridge which marks the northeastern entrance to the development. The houses (Perry, Root, Kier, Ross and Kissam) were all for rent and are named after their first tenant.

JOHN O. CARR HOUSE (1950)
Glenview
This salmon-coloured concrete block house is built to a T-plan. The living room has a patterned concrete block divider from the kitchen.

GEORGE MADISON MILLARD HOUSE (1906)
1689 Lake Avenue, Highland Park
Illustrated on page 99.
A board and batten two-story Prairie house built to a cruciform plan.

MARY M. W. ADAMS HOUSE (1905)
1923 Lake Avenue, Highland Park
Illustrated on page 108.
A plaster-surfaced, wood-framed Prairie style structure built near the shore of Lake Michigan

WARD W. WILLITS HOUSE (1901)
1445 Sheridan Road, Highland Park
Illustrated center left (Gardener's Cottage), above and bottom right (house).
One of the seventeen listed Wright buildings. It's an important building because it shows the culmination of all Wright's feelings about residential architecture. A classic Prairie house constructed from wood and steel with exterior plasterwork and wood trim, the living quarters are all raised above ground level by a chunky stylobate. Each wing of the house comes off a central core in a pinwheel configuration. The end wall of the living room is floor to ceiling glass. The core of the house is a substantial central fireplace. Wright also designed a gardener's cottage and stables behind the house. These are in the wood and plaster structure of the Prairie style.

FREDERICK BAGLEY HOUSE (1894)
121 County Line Road, Hinsdale

This house, like many of Wright's early works, records the tastes of the client rather than Wright. It is built with stained wood shingles (now painted) and a stone veranda. The library is built to an octagonal plan.

WARREN HICKOX HOUSE (1900)
687 South Harrison Avenue, Kankakee
This house illustrates Wright's move to the Prairie style structure where the wood timbers become less obvious than the hither to the popular Tudor style.

B. HARLEY BRADLEY HOUSE (1900)
701 South Harrison Avenue, Kankakee
This house, built to a cruciform plan, is of plaster with wood trim and has leaded-glass windows. Wright also designed a stable. At one time converted into a restaurant, it was renovated for use as offices in 1990.

HIRAM BALDWIN HOUSE (1905)
205 Essex Road, Kenilworth
This Prairie style house has had extensive interior remodeling.

CHARLES F. GLORE HOUSE (1951)
170 North Mayflower, Lake Forest
Illustrated center right.
This is built from an in-line plan and has a children's room opening over the two-story living room. The flues of the fireplaces on both levels share the same masonry core. The building materials are of brick, cypress and salmon concrete block. The building had a much needed renovation in the 1990s.

STEPHEN M. B. HUNT HOUSE (1907)
345 South Seventh Avenue, LaGrange
Illustrated left.
The best built example of "A Fireproof House" (as advertised in 1907). It is a square-plan wood and plaster Prairie style house although it was originally planned to be built of concrete, which would have made it fireproof. Renovation has seen the terraces enclosed but the oak woodwork and the Tiffany brick fireplace have been fully restored.

PETER GOAN HOUSE (1894)
108 South Eighth Avenue, LaGrange
Wright's preference for wood construction of board and batten, laid horizontally, can be clearly seen in this house. The structure has, over the years, lost its original front terrace and second-story porch which gave the house the horizontal character much favoured by Wright at the time.

ROBERT G. EMMOND HOUSE (1892)
109 South Eighth Avenue, LaGrange
Illustrated above
A "bootlegged" T-plan house set sideways to the street. Originally a clapboard structure it has been resurfaced with brick on its lower story. The building has been changed considerably since designed, with its terraces enclosed.

LLOYD LEWIS HOUSE (1939)
153 Little Saint Mary's Road, Libertyville
A two-story building with the living room and a balcony above the ground level bedroom wing and entrance. The building is constructed from brick and cypress. A poultry shed to Wright's 1943 design was added later.

HARRY S. ADAMS HOUSE (1913)
710 Augusta Avenue, Oak Park
Illustrated right.
This is Wright's last work in Oak Park. It is built to a longitudinal plan which runs through the house from porte-cochere through porch, living room and hall to dining room.

FRANK LLOYD WRIGHT HOME AND STUDIO (1889 1911)
951 Chicago Avenue, Oak Park
Illustrated on pages 94 and 95, see Interior Designs section.
Wright's Home and Studio has been much renovated since the 1970s. The Frank Lloyd Wright Home and Studio Foundation takes care of the preservation of these buildings which are listed for preservation by the A.I.A. The Foundation's Oak Park Visitor's Center is at 154 North Forest Avenue. Open to the public, tours are available.

THOMAS H. GALE HOUSE (1892)
1019 Chicago Avenue, Oak Park
A two-story T-plan "Queen Anne" house of clapboard set sideways to the street, was designed while Wright was with Adler & Sullivan.

ROBERT P. PARKER HOUSE (1892)
1027 Chicago Avenue, Oak Park

Identical to 1019 Chicago Avenue (see above).

WALTER H. GALE HOUSE (1893)
1031 Chicago Avenue, Oak Park
Illustrated below right.
The third of the clapboard houses on Chicago Avenue to have been built to identical T-plan (see above 1019 and 1027 Chicago Avenue).

Mrs THOMAS H. GALE HOUSE (1904)
6 Elizabeth Court, Oak Park
Laura Gale's Prairie house which was originally to have been built of concrete. It is built roughly to a square-plan and is often said to be the inspiration for "Fallingwater" (see pages 168 and 170).

ROLLIN FURBECK HOUSE (1897)
515 Fair Oaks Avenue, Oak Park
This three-storied house was built by Wright at the behest of Warren Furbeck for his son. It has a light tan brick and colored wood trim facade and the upper story windows hug the broad overhanging eaves of the hipped roof in a band of stucco.

WILLIAM G. FRICKE HOUSE (1901)
540 Fair Oaks Avenue, Oak Park

Illustrated on pages 71, 101.
A three-story house designed with Webster Tomlinson. Six years after its construction many alterations were made and a garage, in the style of the house, was added. A semi-detached pavilion has been demolished.

FRANK WRIGHT THOMAS HOUSE (1901)
210 Forest Avenue, Oak Park
Illustrated on page 71.
The first of Wright's Prairie style houses to be built in Oak Park. It was commissioned by James C. Rogers for his daughter and son-in-law and is renowned for its art-glass. Nicknamed the "Harem."

PETER A. BEACHY HOUSE (1906)
238 Forest Avenue, Oak Park
Illustrated above left.
This Prairie house incorporates an earlier Gothic style cottage into its structure.

EDWARD R. HILLS/DeCARO HOUSE (1906)
313 Forest Avenue, Oak Park
Illustrated on page 96.
A Prairie house bought by Nathan Moore as a present for daughter Mary and her husband. Tom and Irene DeCaro bought it in 1975 and restored it substantially. Renamed the Hills/DeCaro house in 1977.

ARTHUR HEURTLEY HOUSE (1902)
318 Forest Avenue, Oak Park
Illustrated on pages 96, 100, and 111.
Typical square plan Prairie style house, Heurtley commissioned the house at the same time as his summer cottage in Michigan was being remodeled.

NATHAN G. MOORE HOUSE (1895)
333 Forest Avenue, Oak Park
Illustrated on page 107.
A Roman-brick house which is essentially Tudor in style was rebuilt above the first floor after a fire in 1922. Wright also built the stable. Open to the public, guided tours available during summer months.

Dr. WILLIAM H. COPELAND HOUSE (1909)
400 Forest Avenue, Oak Park
Illustrated on page 69.
Wright extensively altered an existing residence, inside and outside, and built a garage in the Prairie style.

GEORGE W. SMITH HOUSE (1895–8)
404 Home Avenue, Oak Park
Illustrated left.

The use of shingles with this house pre-dates Wright's employment of horizontal board and batten siding which were to become the trademark of his numerous Prairie and Usonian buildings.

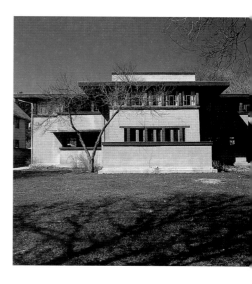

UNITY TEMPLE (1904)
Lake Street at Kenilworth Avenue, Oak Park
Illustrated on pages 102 and 103.
Another building listed by the A.I.A., the church is considered to be the first significant American building to use poured concrete, which was in part dictated by the need to keep the costs down. Severe on the outside, inside it is richly decorated. Stairs to upper level are contained in the pylons at the four corners. Open to the public, guided tours available.

HARRISON P. YOUNG HOUSE (1895)
334 North Kenilworth Avenue, Oak Park
Wright extensively remodeled this house, moving the structure back 16ft.

OSCAR B. BALCH HOUSE (1911)
611 North Kenilworth Avenue, Oak Park
Illustrated above right.
A plaster-surfaced, wood-trimmed Prairie house. The original dark brown wood trim on white plaster (Wright's preferred color scheme) has been modified to an orange tinted wood trim on gray plaster.

GEORGE W. FURBECK HOUSE (1897)
223 North Euclid Avenue, Oak Park
Illustrated below right.
Only the brown brick and wood trim remain from the original of this house. The porch has been enlarged and enclosed thus greatly altering Wright's proportions.

CHARLES ROBERTS HOUSE (1896)
317 and 321 North Euclid Avenue, Oak Park
Wright was retained by Charles Roberts to remodel his house and its stables.

EDWIN H. CHENEY HOUSE (1903)
520 North East Avenue, Oak Park
Illustrated on pages 97, 104 and 105.
A single story brick and wood-trim house with a brick wall enclosed terrace. House where Wright met Mamah Cheney. Over 50 examples of art-glass. In 1997 it was being used as a bed and breakfast establishment.

HARRY C. GOODRICH HOUSE (1895)
534 North East Avenue, Oak Park
Illustrated on page 100.
This two-story house still has the original light colored clapboards. The

second story windows are located directly below the eaves and the lower boards conceal a basement built partially above the ground. The original open porch has now been enclosed.

WILLIAM E. MARTIN HOUSE (1903)
636 North East Avenue, Oak Park
Illustrated above.

A three-story house of plaster and wood-trim and a precursor of the Prairie houses to come. The building was restored to a single family house in 1945 after many years of being split into three apartments. Originally landscaped by Burley Griffin, little of this now remains.

FRANCIS J. WOOLLEY HOUSE (1893)
1030 Superior Street, Oak Park

This house has been resurfaced with an imitation brick siding quite likely covering its original clapboards.

FRANCIS W. LITTLE HOUSE (1902)
1505 West Moss, Peoria

Wright was commissioned to design a brick T-plan house with a spacious separate stable. The house was enlarged in 1909 when additions elongated the original T-plan. The porch has subsequently been enclosed by glass.

ROBERT MUIRHEAD HOUSE (1950)
Rohrsen Road, Plato Center

An elongated plan built on a four-foot module. The main building materials of this one story house consist of common brick and cypress.

E. ARTHUR DAVENPORT HOUSE (1901)
559 Ashland Avenue, River Forest

This two-story house was a Webster Tomlinson collaboration. It is a stained wood board and batten structure with plaster under the eaves of a gable roof. Its original front terrace has subsequently been removed. Executed using Wright's second design for *The Ladies' Home Journal*.

WILLIAM H. WINSLOW HOUSE (1893)
515 Auvergne Place, River Forest

The house features the architect's early octagonal geometry using the basic materials of Roman brick, stone and plaster. The two-story building was Wright's first independent commission.

CHAUNCEY L. WILLIAMS HOUSE (1895)
530 Edgewood Place, River Forest
Illustrated below left.

A two-story building with a steeply pitched roof. The house features Roman brick built beneath the sill line, which is colorfully offset by the plaster between the eaves.

ISABEL ROBERTS HOUSE (1908)
603 Edgewood Place, River Forest, Illinois
Illustrated on page 97.

This building, designed to a cruciform plan, was originally constructed of wood and plaster surface. It is a Prairie with the usual two-story high living room. The house was remodeled in 1955 when it was resurfaced with brick veneer using Philippine mahogany for the interior modifications. The south porch of the building is built around a tree.

J. KIBBEN INGALLS HOUSE (1909)
562 Keystone Avenue, River Forest, Illinois
Illustrated above right.

This building is the last of Wright's existing work in River Forest. It is a typical Prairie style house of plastered surface and wood trim.

RIVER FOREST TENNIS CLUB (1906)
615 Lathrop Avenue, River Forest, Illinois
Illustrated below right.

Today the building reveals little of Wright's original contribution which was a horizontal board and batten construction.

AVERY COONLEY PRIVATE PLAYHOUSE (1912)
350 Fairbanks Road, Riverside
Illustrated center right.

Built to a symmetrical plan, this post-Prairie design is now significantly altered from the original. The clerestory windows, designed by Wright in multi-coloured geometrical designs, are no longer fully intact.

F. F. TOMEK HOUSE (1907)
150 Nuttell Road, Riverside

This house was bulit to a L-plan. It is a Prairie style house with a small second-story built over the large main floor. The supports now seen to the terrace roof are a later additon. It was the prototype for the Robie House.

AVERY COONLEY HOUSE (1907)
300 Scottswood Road, Riverside
Illustrated above and on page 110.

The house is Wright's first work using the zoned plan. Inlaid tiles are used to form a geometrical pattern on the plaster-surfaced, wood-trimmed house. It has raised living quarters in the Prairie style with a pavilion linking the various spaces. The gardener's cottage (290, Scotswood Road) was built in 1911 and the coach house, originally a stable, the same year. Both buildings were featured in the original published plans but were constructed later. The residence has now been converted into three separate apartments and the coach house is on a separate plot (336 Coonley Road).

KEN LAURENT HOUSE (1949)
Spring Brook Road, Rockford

This is a single-story Usonian solar hemicycle constructed from common brick and cypress. The plan incorporates special access facilities for the disabled owner, Ken Laurent.

THE DANA-THOMAS HOUSE
(SUSAN LAWRENCE DANA HOUSE [1902] AND LAWRENCE MEMOR-IAL LIBRARY [1905])

301-327 East Lawrence Avenue, Springfield
Illustrated above, right and on pages 92–93.

The house is of cruciform plan and it incorporates a former house into its brick structure. It is a Prairie style house and is the first example of Wright's work to feature his characteristic two-story high living room. The house is connected to the library by means of a covered passage that doubled as a conservatory. As befitted an art collector, there is much art-glass and sculptures by Richard Bock. It was bought and restored by Mr. and Mrs. Charles C. Thomas in 1944. Both house and library are open to the public and tours are available.

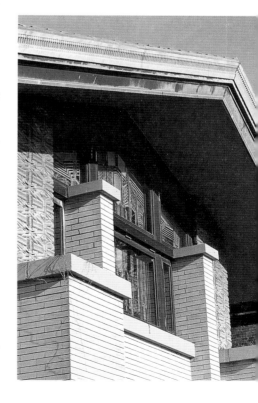

FRANK J. BAKER (1909)
507 Lake Avenue, Wilmette
Illustrated below left.

The plan for the ground floor is cruciform with a second-story L-plan. The building is a Prairie style wood house with plaster surface and features the characteristic two story high living room. As with many of Wright's houses, the once open porches are now enclosed.

ABOVE and RIGHT: The
Dana-Thomas House.
See page 91.

Different views of the
Frank Lloyd Wright
Home and Studio. See
page 86.

ABOVE: The Heurtley House. See page 86.

LEFT: The Cheney House. This was the project FLW was working on when he met and fell in love with Mamah Cheney Borthwick. See page 87.

BELOW LEFT: The Isabel Roberts House. See page 89.

FAR LEFT: The Hills/DeCaro House. See page 86.

ABOVE, RIGHT, and FAR RIGHT, The Pettit Memorial Chapel. See page 75.

ABOVE: The George Millard House. See page 82.

ABOVE: The Goodrich
House. See page 87.

RIGHT: The Heurtley
House, See page 86.

100

RIGHT and BELOW: The Fricke House. See pages 85–86.

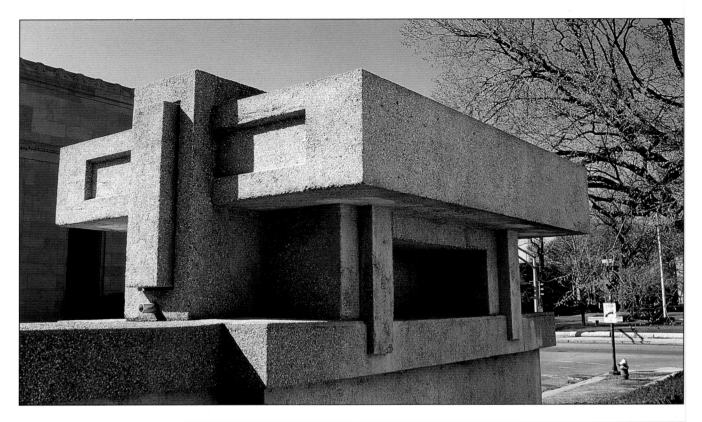

THIS PAGE and FAR
RIGHT: All views of
Unity Temple. See page
87.

THIS PAGE and OPPO-
SITE: The Cheney House.
See page 87.

RIGHT and BELOW
RIGHT: The Blossom
House. See page 76.

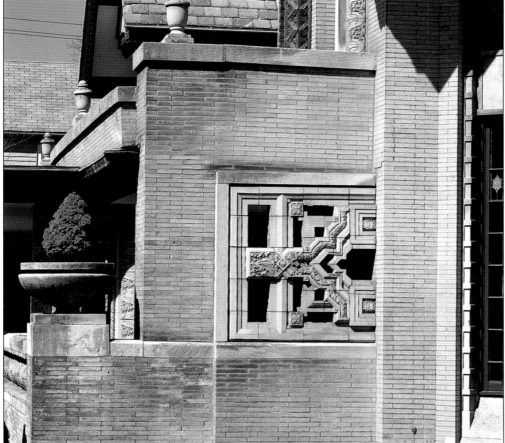

ABOVE and LEFT: The
Nathan Moore House.
See page 86.

RIGHT and FAR RIGHT:
The Charnley House.
See page 75.

BELOW: The Mary
Adams House. See page
82.

ABOVE: Horse Show Fountain replica in Scoville Park, Oak Park.

ABOVE and BELOW LEFT: Interiors of the Arthur Heurtley House. See page 86.

OPPOSITE, ABOVE and BELOW: The Coonley House. See page 90.

I O W A

Wright designed two buildings in Iowa before he left for Europe with Mamah Cheney. The first — the Stockman House — was one of the houses which developed from his article "A Fireproof House for $5000" that was published in *The Ladies' Home Journal* in April 1907. In the article, the houses designed around these plans (like the Hunt House in LaGrange, Illinois; see page 84) were originally intended to be made from poured concrete, a building medium that Wright pioneered effectively in the Unity Temple, Oak Park in 1904. In reality, the medium was too expensive for this sized dwelling, and brick and plaster were used instead. A year later, in Mason City, he started work on the City National Bank Building and Hotel, a job he left to be finished by William Drummond. It would be nearly forty years before he saw another of his designs built in Iowa, a gap caused by

ABOVE LEFT, ABOVE, and LEFT: City National Bank Building. See page 114.

the opprobrium of his personal life, the Great Depression and the building restrictions enforced during the Second World War. Indeed, it would not be until 1950 that the Walter House, designed by 1945, could be lived in. His other buildings in Iowa are all private residences, the construction of last ones taking place after Wright's death in 1959.

DOUGLAS GRANT HOUSE (1946)
3400 Adel Drive S.E., Cedar Rapids
This is a long I-plan two-story house built from local stone with a reinforced concrete roof, flagstone floors, and a copper fascia. It is built on a slope so the entrance is on the second story.

ALVIN MILLER HOUSE (1946)
1107 Court Street, Charles City
A single-story, L-plan house with a clerestory, on the Cedar River.

PAUL J. TRIER HOUSE (1956)
6880 North West Beaver Drive, Des Moines
A late design, this is a single-story wood-trimmed building with additions in 1960.

ROBERT T. SUNDAY HOUSE (1955)
Woodfield Road, Marshalltown
Designed by Wright as an L-plan Usonian house, with a substantial living room, it had a 1970 addition giving it a T-plan. One of the last brick Usonian homes, construction was undertaken after Wright's death by John H. Howe, who also designed the later addition.

G. C. STOCKMAN HOUSE (1908)
First Street N.E., at E. State, Mason City
Illustrated above left and right.
This two-story, dark-wood-banded Prairie house, Wright's earliest building in Iowa, was moved to its current location in 1989 and restored. It is almost identical to the Hunt House (see page 84). The house is open to the public for much of the year.

CITY NATIONAL BANK AND HOTEL (1909)
5 West State Street, Mason City
Illustrated on pages 112 and 113.
Designed by Wright for J.E.E. Markley, whom he had met at his aunt's Hillside Home School, construction was finished under the guidance of William Drummond while Wright was in Europe. Both the bank and the Park Inn Hotel behind it have been substantially altered over the years — particularly by the insertion (as illustrated) of shop windows in the bank's side. Open to the public during normal working hours.

CARROLL ALSOP HOUSE designed (1948) built (1951)
1907 A Avenue East, Oskaloosa
An L-plan single-story house with an angled main bedroom. Built of brick and cypress with a red shingled roof.

JACK LAMBERSON HOUSE designed (1948) built (1951)
511 North Park Avenue, Oskaloosa
A spectacular brick and redwood single-story building near the Alsop House, with a big triangular carport.

LOWELL WALTER HOUSE (1945) **AND RIVER PAVILION** (1948)
2611 Quasqueton Diag. Boulevard, Quasqueton
Illustrated below and right (House), pages 117–18 (River Pavilion).
The main house, which Wright's called his "Opus 497" — what he roughly reckoned to be the number of designs he had produced by 1945 — is a Usonian I-plan brick and steel construction with the garden/living room turned to give better views of the Wapsipinicon River. The pavilion, sited further down the hill on the river, is a brick boathouse with a sun-terrace and room above. It was restored in 1991. The house is open to the public during the summer months.

K A N S A S

Another state with designs separated by forty years, Kansas can boast a substantial residence for a political hopeful in the form of the Henry Allen House, and an impressively utilitarian university building.

JUVENILE CULTURAL STUDY CENTER (1957)
Wichita State University,
North Yale Avenue at 21st Street, Wichita
Illustrated above and right.
Known as the Harry F. Corbin Education Center, as it was Corbin who was president of the University of Wichita and the prime mover in getting Wright for this project, the Center is one of two buildings planned for the site. The second, a laboratory, was never built. The Center has two,

THE JUVENILE
CULTURAL STUDY
CENTER.

ABOVE: Atrium and
north wing.

LEFT: North wing from
the central roof terrace.

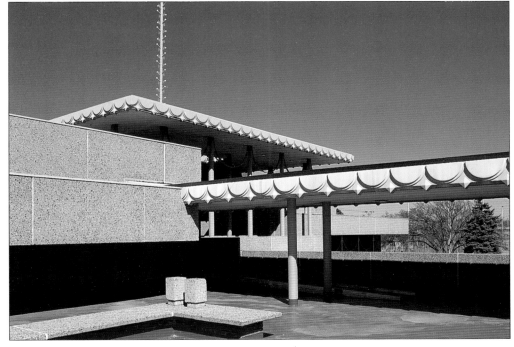

ABOVE: View of the Allen House looking west, with porte cochere at left and living room at right.

RIGHT: Allen House living room.

two, two-story, rectangular units on either side of a patio enlivened by a fountain and esplanade. Each unit has an atrium where it meets the central units (as illustrated). Constructed from cast concrete, the building contains classrooms and offices, and has a roof terrace. The center is open to visitors while the university is open.

HENRY J. ALLEN HOUSE (1917)
255 North Roosevelt Boulevard, Wichita, Kansas
Illustrated above, left and on pages 124 and 125.

This is Wright's only private house in Kansas — but what a house! Built for presidential hopeful Henry Allen, governor of Kansas 1919–23, the exterior appearance of a brick Prairie house hides the enclosed garden, terrace, pool, and summer house. Bequeathed by the second owner to Wichita State University in the 1980s, it was subsequently sold to the Allen-Lambe House Association. It is now open to the public and guided tours are available by appointment.

RIGHT and FAR RIGHT:
The Allen House — interior details. See page 123.

KENTUCKY

Wright's only work in Kentucky is said to have been secured while he was in Europe with Mamah Cheney, when they met Presbyterian minister Jessie Ziegler.

REV. J. R. ZIEGLER HOUSE (1909)
509 Shelby Street, Frankfort

The building is a two-story Prairie style structure with interesting Wrightian interior design (sideboards, bookcases, etc.). The house has had the back porch enclosed and built upon (another bedroom). Guided tours are available by appointment.

MARYLAND

There are only two examples of Wright's work in Maryland and both show his talent for drawing the best from difficult terrain and locations. The Euchtman House was built on a difficult, overlooked lot. Wright built into the slope, effectively presenting the neighbor to the north with a view of carport and the rear of the house, freeing the private southern arc. For his son Llewellyn's house, he made the best use of a ravine running around the southwest of the property to provide a dramatic profile.

JOSEPH EUCHTMAN HOUSE (1939)
6807 Cross Country Boulevard, Baltimore

A Usonian I-plan building, the main feature of this two-bedroom house is the living room, which opens onto both a southwest-facing terrace shaded by the extended roof, and also onto a southeast-facing deck inserted after construction had been completed.

ROBERT LLEWELLYN WRIGHT HOUSE (1953)
7927 Deepwell Drive, Bethesda

This two-story concrete-block hemicycle was built for Wright's sixth child, Robert Llewellyn Wright. With a stunning second-story balcony coming off the master bedroom and a cantilevered porch, it perches over a ravine, with a southwest-facing terrace and pool.

M A S S A C H U S E T T S

Wright's only work in Massachusetts is a single story I-plan house with detached shop built in 1940.

THEODORE BAIRD HOUSE (1940)
38 Shays Street, Amherst

This is a typical Usonian brick house with horizontal cypress board and sunk batten. Internally, it has an interesting back-to-back double fire arrangement in the living room and a specially built indentation in the living room wall to take an upright piano.

M I C H I G A N

Because of Michigan's proximity to Illinois where Wright studied, lived, and did most of his early work, there are a great many examples of his buildings. Wright's first work in Michigan was the "Bridge Cottage" in Whitehall built in 1902. Interestingly for a man who did so much writing, proof of the success of this "advertising" comes from the number of people who came to Wright after seeing publications by or about him. Examples from Michigan are Mel and Sara Smith, who fell in love with the architecture they saw in the special June 1938 issue of *Architectural Forum* devoted to Wright, and Dorothy Turkel, who contacted Wright after reading *The Natural House*. She and her husband Dr. H. Turkel ended up with the only built two-story Usonian "automatic"

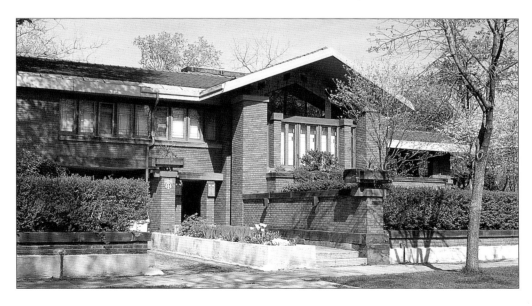

LEFT: The Amberg House. See page 130.

house. Michigan also contains two estate developments (and a house from a third — Usonia I), which show well the way that Wright's designs lent themselves to mass-production, both in the simplicity of their construction — for example, the use of concrete blocks — and in the way that basic designs could be modified to suit individual requirements and the geography of the site. The two estates were the Galesburg Country Homes, the concept of a group of chemists working together in a company in Kalamazoo, and Parkwyn Village, created by some of the same people involved with the Galesburg plan but who decided that a site nearer their work was in order. Unfortunately, few of the planned houses were built, but from what was constructed we can get a small idea of how the residential sections of Broadacre City would have looked.

WILLIAM PALMER HOUSE (1950)
227 Orchard Hills Drive, Ann Arbor
Bill Palmer was Professor of Mathematics at the University of Michigan and chose Wright to design his home. He got a single-story Usonian house, built to a triangular plan that complements perfectly the hilltop on which it rests.

HOWARD E. ANTHONY HOUSE (1949)
1150 Miami Road, Benton Harbor
Illustrated above right.
With views over the St. Joseph River, this single-story stone building is trimmed with cypress and has a roof of cedar shingles.

GREGOR S. AFFLECK HOUSE (1940)
1925 North Woodward Avenue, Bloomfield Hills
Today owned by the Lawrence Institute of Technology, who restored the house in the 1980s, the Affleck House is another example of Wright's ability to maximize the dramatic settings of his houses. One of Affleck's relatives was Wright's secretary at Taliesin and he spent much time in his youth in Spring Green. It is unsurprising, therefore, that he chose Wright to build his home. The living room (interior flawlessly restored) is built on piers, cantilevered over a basement and garden level, which has seats and a pool. Guided tours by appointment only.

MELVIN MAXWELL SMITH HOUSE (1949)
5045 Pon Valley Road, Bloomfield Hills
Enlarged by Taliesin Associated Architects in 1969-70, this is an L-plan Usonian brick and batten single-story house. Mel Smith acted as his own contractor because two teachers' salaries (his and his wife Sara's) could not stretch to cover the cost in the immediate postwar years.

DOROTHY H. TURKEL HOUSE (1955)
2760 West Seven Mile Road, Detroit
An L-plan Usonian "automatic" construction with a two-story living

room. There are no windows; light is admitted through floor-to-ceiling pierced blocks.

ERIC PRATT HOUSE (1948)
11036 Hawthorne Drive, Galesberg
GALESBERG COUNTRY HOMES The westernmost block of the homes is a long I-plan textile-block "automatic" house with central living room. Pratt was the general purchasing agent for the homes.

SAMUEL EPPSTEIN HOUSE (1948)
11098 Hawthorne Drive, Galesberg
GALESBERG COUNTRY HOMES Constructed as No. 11036, the Eppstein House is dug deeply into the hillside with the living room opening out into a large north-facing terrace.

CURTIS MEYER HOUSE (1950)
11108 Hawthorne Drive, Galesberg
GALESBERG COUNTRY HOMES East-facing solar hemicycle built from concrete block.

DAVID I. WEISBLAT HOUSE(1948)
11185 Hawthorne Drive, Galesberg
GALESBERG COUNTRY HOMES Enlarged by the Taliesin Associated Architects in 1960. The first of the four Galesberg homes, it is built to a T-plan employing Wright's textile-block and wood construction. The living room roof is cantilevered, to maximize living room window space.

ERNEST VOSBURGH SUMMER HOUSE (1916)
46208 Crescent Road, Grand Beach
This Prairie house is the only one of the three that Wright designed in Grand Beach that remains much as built. It has a two-story living room and looks out toward Lake Michigan.

JOSEPH J. BAGLEY SUMMER HOUSE (1916)
47017 Lakeview, Grand Beach
This summer house overlooking Lake Michigan is a two-story unit spreading into single-story wings. It has been much altered from the original Wright design.

W. S. CARR SUMMER HOUSE (1916)
46039 Lakeview, Grand Beach
Four-bedroom vacation house on Lake Michigan.

J. H. AMBERG HOUSE (1909)
505 College Avenue S.E. Grand Rapids
Illustrated on page 127.
This house's attribution has been questioned. It seems likely that Wright did the preliminary work before going to Europe in 1910, leaving the design and construction to be finished by van Holst and Marion Mahoney.

MEYER MAY HOUSE (1908) extended (1920)
450 Madison Avenue, S.E. Grand Rapids
Illustrated right.
A superb T-plan two-story Prairie house built with Roman brick. Its interior boasts much art-glass and a Niedecken mural. May was Amberg's son-in-law and suggested Wright for the Amberg House. Restored 1987–88 it is now open to the public

WARD McCARTNEY HOUSE (1949)
2662 Taliesin Drive, Kalamazoo
Illustrated above left.
PARKWYN VILLAGE Built on a diamond (double equilateral triangle) module. The single-story house is built with Wright "textile-block" and mahogany. Although the enclosure of the north portal and a carport came later, they were part of Wright's original plan.

ERIC V. BROWN HOUSE (1949)
2806 Taliesin Drive, Kalamazoo
Illustrated below left and on page 133.
PARKWYN VILLAGE One of the four houses built at Parkwyn Village, although several more were designed in the original master plan. A single-story house overlooking Lorenz Lake, it was built with Wright "textile-block" and mahogany. The living room has a terrace attached.

ROBERT LEVIN HOUSE (1948) extended (1960)
2816 Taliesin Drive, Kalamazoo
PARKWYN VILLAGE A single-story house built with Wright "textile-block" and cypress. There is a later (1960) addition by John H. Howe of the Taliesin Associated Architects, who was also the construction supervisor of the Wright homes at Parkwyn.

ROBERT WINN HOUSE (1950)
2822 Taliesin Drive, Kalamazoo
PARKWYN VILLAGE The only two-story house in Parkwyn Village, the Winn House has a breathtaking curved, cantilevered, enclosed, skylighted balcony attached to its living room. It is built with Wright "textile-block" and wood.

ABBY BEECHER ROBERTS HOUSE (1936)
"Deertrack," County Highway 492, Marquette
A single-story house in a forest, it has a northeast-facing living room that is glazed on three sides. Mrs. Roberts was the mother-in-law of an architect who trained at Taliesin in the 1930s.

ARTHUR HEURTLEY SUMMER COTTAGE remodelling (1902)
Les Cheneaux Club, Marquette Island
On the shores of Lake Huron, this cottage was remodeled by Wright at the same time as he was involved with the Heurtley House in Oak Park (see page 86).

AMY ALPAUGH STUDIO (1947)
71 North Peterson Park Road, Northport
A single-story house with views over Lake Michigan, it is built of, primarily, brick, oak, and ash. It's most obvious asset is the southwest-facing studio/living room. The house has seen alterations — the porch has been enclosed to form an extra room, there's a playroom where Amy Alpaugh used to keep goats, and the greenhouse has become a bedroom.

JAMES EDWARDS HOUSE (1949)
2504 Arrow Head Road, Okemos
Edwards wrote to Wright in 1948 after seeing an article in *The House Beautiful*. He received a pleasant red brick and cypress design with a glazed west-facing living room and a terrace along the length of the west wall. Additions were made by the Taliesin Associated Architects in 1968.

ERLING P. BRAUNER HOUSE (1948)
2527 Arrow Head Road, Okemos
Close to the Edwards House is this single-story adaptation of the Usonian concept with "textile-block" replacing brick.

GOETSCH-WINCKLER HOUSE (1939)
2410 Hulett Road, Okemos
This Usonian house was built for two ladies from the University of Michigan Art Department. It was the only one built of a development known as Usonia I, which was to have been a venture between various teachers at what was then called the Michigan Agricultural College. It has an 18-foot cantilevered carport roof, and the bedrooms open out onto a private, enclosed, lanai.

DONALD SCHABERG HOUSE (1950) addition (1960s)
1155 Wrightwind Drive, Okemos
An large house with the 1960s addition of a family room and bedroom designed by original construction supervisor, Wright's ubiquitous John H. Howe.

LEWIS W. GODDARD HOUSE (1953)
12221 Beck Road, Plymouth
A friend of Carlton Wall, whose house is just to the south, Goddard's single-story brick and wood house has an extended carport and a substantial living room, that is glazed on its north, east, and south-facing sides.

CARLTON D. WALL HOUSE (1941)
"Snowflake," 12305 Beck Road, Plymouth
Called "Snowflake" by Wright because of its hexagonal grid, the house is constructed from brick and cypress. The living room, with its cantilevered roof, opens out onto a walled, east-facing, terrace and there is an enclosed patio.

CARL SCHULTZ HOUSE (1957)
2704 Highland Court, Saint Joseph
Completed by the Taliesin Associated Architects after Wright's death, the Schultz House was built from reused bricks from the owners other properties in the area. It looks out over the St. Joseph River and has a massive cantilevered terrace and a large basement.

INA MORRIS HARPER HOUSE (1950)
207 Sunnybank, Saint Joseph
A single-story house of "Chicago common" brick overlooking Lake Michigan, Mrs. Harper had read about Wright in an article in *House Beautiful*. The living room opens out onto a west-facing terrace.

GEORGE GERTS DUPLEX (1902)
"Bridge Cottage," 5260 South Shore Drive, Whitehall
With a bridged loggia over Birch Brook which flows into nearby White Lake, this beautiful duplex has had a second-floor sleeping area added.

THOMAS H. GALE SUMMER HOUSES (1897)
5318 South Shore Drive, Whitehall
Thomas Gale and George Gerts had married two sisters and bought up adjoining lots of White Lake land for summer cottages with easy access to Lake Michigan and, therefore, Chicago. This was the first to be built and is much altered.

Mrs THOMAS H. GALE SUMMER HOUSES (1905)
5324, 5370, and 5380 South Shore Drive, Whitehall
The summer house is a two-story board and batten cottage. Two nearly identical units were built on nearby plots but only one of them remains in good condition.

LEFT: The Brown House. See page 130.

133

MINNESOTA

Wright's earliest extant building in Minnesota, the 1933-designed 255 Bedford Street — the Malcolm E. Willey House — represents a major link between Wright's Prairie and Usonian styles. Most of the components were there: the workspace central and directly adjoining the living room; the radiator floor heating, a direct forerunner of the gravity heating characteristc of the Usonian home. Twenty-two years later, in 1955, one of the last Usonian houses was built in Stillwater. Minnesota can also lay claim to the only service station constructed from Wright's designs. The design derives from the Broadacre City Standardized Overhead Service Station of 1932, except that ground based pumps are used instead of the overhead fuel lines envisaged by Wright.

In 1957 one of Wright's designs for the Marshall Erdman Company for a prefabricated structure was built in Rochester. Wright conceived

three different prefabricated designs with Marshal Erdman, but only two were ever realized albeit in reasonable numbers, and this house represents the original of the second of those. This version of the "one room house" is a wood structure based on the "textile-block" "automatic" Usonian.

ABOVE: Fasbender Medical Center. See page 136.

S. P. ELAY HOUSE (1950)
309 21st Street S.W., Austin
This two-story house is one of the largest late Usonian houses and is built of stone and cypress. It has an additional garage and rear terrace which are not part of Wright's original design.

R. W. LINDHOLM HOUSE (1952)
Route 33 at Stanley Avenue, Cloquet
Built before his service station, the Lindholm House is a T plan that opens the bedrooms and living roon to the west. It is constructed from painted concrete block and wood-trim.

R. W. LINDHOLM SERVICE STATION (1957)
Route 45 at Route 33, Cloquet
Illustrated above.

Wright's only built service station, it is constructed from painted cement block with a terne metal roof and cantilevered canopy. Open during working hours. Tours available by appointment.

HERMAN T. FASBENDER MEDICAL CLINIC (1957)
State Highway 55 at Pine Street, Hastings
Illustrated on pages 134 and 135.

This one-story building is constructed from brick with a copper roof. It is currently used as office premises. Open during working hours.

MALCOLM E. WILLEY HOUSE (1933)
255 Bedford Street S.E., Minneapolis

A single-story house which represents a major link between Wright's Prairie style houses and his later Usonian house plan, having the kitchen directly adjoining the living room. It is constructed from dark red sand and paving brick, with cypress wood-trim.

HARRY J. NEILS HOUSE (1949)
2801 Burnham Boulevard, Minneapolis

This house on Cedar Lake was commissioned by someone who worked in metal and stone and could acquire them — which accounts for Wright being able to use building materials like scrap marble and aluminum window framing. The house is dominated by a large chimney and the east-facing terrace which opens off the living room.

A. H. BULBULIAN HOUSE (1947)
1229 Skyline Drive S.W., Rochester
A one-story house built on the brow of a hill and constructed from cement brick and cypress.

THOMAS E. KEYS HOUSE (1950)
1243 Skyline Drive S.W., Rochester
A single-story house built from concrete block with pine wood-trim. The 1971 additions enlarged the living room and converted the former carport into an en suite guest room.

JAMES B. MACBEAN HOUSE (1957)
1532 Woodland Drive S.W., Rochester
One of the Marshall Erdman Company No. 2 Prefabs, this house, set into a hillside, is essentially a square-plan "one-room house". It is constructed from concrete block and painted horizontal board and batten.

PAUL OLFELT HOUSE (1958)
226 Parkland Lane, Saint Louis Park
This small house is built into a hillside; the living room opens out to a downhill aspect, and the west-facing deck off the living room is therefore supported from below. Construction was completed by the Taliesin Associated Architects after Wright's death.

DONALD LOVNESS HOUSE (1955) **COTTAGE** (1958–76)
10121 83rd North, Stillwater
Illustrated below, above right, and on pages 138, 139.
This single-story structure is one of the last Usonian houses. It is constructed from stone and wood. The master and guest bedrooms form separate wings. The cottage is a square plan "one-room cottage" with a central fireplace in the living room.

THIS PAGE and OPPO-
SITE: The Lovness
House. See page 137.

M I S S O U R I

Wright's buildings in Missouri split neatly into two eras — immediately pre-war and the early 1950s. The Bott House is certainly the most dramatic of the mainly residential commissions, and the Community Christian Church the most disappointing when compared to Wright's original drawings.

CLARENCE SONDERN HOUSE (1940)
3600 Bellview Avenue, Kansas City
Originally a standard Usonian house, and the first for which John H. Howe supervised construction, the 1948 additional work transformed it completely, adding a large living area a quarter-story below the original design.

KANSAS CITY COMMUNITY CHRISTIAN CHURCH (1940)
4601 Main Street, Kansas City
Illustrated right and on pages 142 and 143.
There were problems during the construction of the church, generally caused by differences of opinion between the client and Wright, who wanted to use pressure-sprayed concrete. The "light-towers" were blacked out during wartime, but can still be seen working (see illustration). Open to the public. Guided tours available by appointment.

FRANK BOTT HOUSE (1956)
3640 North Briarcliff Road, Kansa City
Built from desert "rubblestone" acquired from the local flinthills and trimmed with Philippine mahogany, the house is seen at its dramatic best looking north from the ravine. From here the jutting terrace, a cantilevered living room and balcony, can be seen to good effect. Construction finished in 1962, under supervision from the Taliesin Associated Architects

RUSSELL W. M. KRAUS HOUSE (1951)
120 North Ballas Road, Kirkwood
A Usonian house with interesting art-glass manufactured by the owner. There is both a lanai and a substantial walled terrace.

T. A. PAPPAS HOUSE (1955)
865 South Masonridge Road, Saint Louis
A Usonian "automatic" design, constructed from salmon-tinted blocks which the owner assembled himself.

M I S S I S S I P P I

In 1890, while Wright was working for Louis Sullivan, he was delegated to undertake the work for Sullivan's summer residence at Ocean Springs. Sullivan had acquired the land from his friends (and clients) the Charnleys, for whom the Adler & Sullivan company undertook a Chicago townhouse (see page 75) as well as a summer house, like Sullivan's, looking out towards the Gulf of Mexico. They were to be Wright's only commissions in Mississippi until the post-war years when, in 1948, he designed "Fountainhead" (306 Glenway Drive, Jackson). This is a house which gives the only example of modern Wright architecture in the state. The building represents a complete demonstration of organic principles in design. Wright proclaimed that the structural principles found in natural forms should guide modern American architecture and put his words into practice at "Fountainhead."

J. WILLIS HUGHES HOUSE (1948)
"Fountainhead," 306 Glenway Drive, Jackson
A Usonian house with two wings splayed at 120° to each other, "Fountainhead" was made from poured concrete. The name comes from the pool and fountain which open off the western, bedroom wing. The northern wing ends in a glazed living room and terrace. Serious remedial action had to be taken in the 1980s after neglect.

LOUIS SULLIVAN SUMMER HOUSE AND STABLES (1890)
100 Holcomb Boulevard, Ocean Springs
The original T-plan was altered by the 1970 addition of a new dining room. The high-pitched roof is characteristic of Wright's early work and the woodwork in the rooms remains in good condition despite the many alterations made during the restoration in the 1930s. The stables were demolished in 1942.

JAMES CHARNLEY SUMMER HOUSE AND GUESTHOUSE (1890)
507 and 509 East Beach, Ocean Springs
The main residence is built to a T-plan, featuring bay windows of octagonal geometry. The house was restored in the 1930s and alterations included replacing the front wooden steps by brick. As with a lot of Wright's work, the porches have been enclosed. The guest house was built to a large octagon divided by a single wall into two rooms.

MONTANA

Fifty years separate Wright's two buildings in Montana — the substantial but ill-fated Como Orchard project, and the Kundert clinic of Opthalmology.

COMO ORCHARD SUMMER COLONY (1908)
Bunkhouse Road, Darby
Today mostly demolished, the Como Orchard Summer Colony at one time had fourteen buildings from Wright's designs including clubhouse, manager's office, and various cottages. Only two cottages remain.

KUNDERT MEDICAL CLINIC (1958)
341 Central Avenue, Whitefish
Commissioned by two doctors — Kundert and Fogo who knew of Wright as they had come from La Crosse, Wisconsin, and Richland Center respectively — the design of this clinic of Opthalmology is based on Usonian principles. It is open during working hours.

NEBRASKA

A 1905 Prairie house built in McCook is Wright's only work in Nebraska. It has been restored extensively by Donald J. Poore.

HARVEY P. SUTTON HOUSE (1905)
602 Norris Avenue, McCook, Nebraska
This Prairie style house is Wright's only work in Nebraska. It is the usual plaster-surfaced wood-trimmed construction.

NEW HAMPSHIRE

The two examples of Wright's work in New Hampshire were built within shouting distance of each other, about five years apart.

TOUFIC H. KALIL HOUSE (1955)
117 Heather Street, Manchester
Illustrated above.
This Usonian "automatic" house is built to an L plan extended to a T with the addition of a carport.

ISADORE J. ZIMMERMAN HOUSE (1950)
223 Heather Street, Manchester
Illustrated right and on pages 148, 149, 213, and 216.
This long single-story house has a clerestory lighting the living room. It is mainly constructed from brick. Guided tours by appointment only.

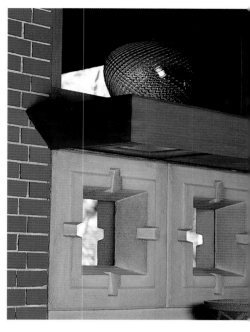

THIS PAGE and OPPO-
SITE: The Zimmermann
House. See page 146.

NEW JERSEY

The four examples of Wright's work in the state of New Jersey are all private houses and span a period of fourteen years from 1940 (the Christie House) to 1954 (the Wilson House).

JAMES B. CHRISTIE HOUSE (1940)
190 Jockey Hollow Road, Bernardsville
A single-story house built to an L plan. The living space occupies the end of one of the legs.

J. A. SWEETON HOUSE (1950)
375 Kings Highway, Cherry Hill
The house is built to a T plan using a four-foot square module. It is constructed with a red concrete-slab floor with interior redwood plywood board and batten. The red roof, originally laid out in overlapping boards, is now covered with asbestos shingles. It has a cantilevered fireplace and carport.

STUART RICHARDSON HOUSE (1941)
63 Chestnut Hill Place, Glen Ridge
This brick-built Usonian house represents an early example of Wright's use of triangular forms.

ABRAHAM WILSON HOUSE (1954) additions (1970)
142 S. River Road, Millstone
This house has a two-story living room with bedrooms over the kitchen. It is constructed from concrete block with wood trim.

NEW MEXICO

The only example of Wright's work in the state of New Mexico is the "Fir Tree," a summer residence in Pecos.

ARNOLD FREEMAN SUMMER HOUSE (1945)
"The Fir Tree," Pecos
Wright's only house in New Mexico is constructed with desert "rubble-stone" walls with trim and roof of rough cedar shakes

RIGHT: The Solomon R. Guggenheim Museum, New York. See page 155.

N E W   Y O R K

Examples of Wright's work in New York state range from private homes, including a Marshall Erdman Company Prefab, to an auto showroom, and one of his best-known and greatest achievements, the Guggenheim Museum. His earliest work is in Buffalo with four private residences built between 1903 and 1908; also from1908 there's a classic Prairie house in Rochester. It was to be nearly twenty years before his next New York commission "Graycliff", a summer house and garage, at Lakeshore, Derby, in 1927 and a further ten years before the Ben Rebhuhn House. After the Second World War, between 1948 and 1951, three Usonian houses were built closely together in wooded, hilly countryside within

ABOVE and LEFT: The George Barton House. See page 154.

commuting distance north of New York City at Pleasantville — the "Usonia Homes" complex, for which Wright was engaged to design himself, or approve the design of, all the houses proposed for the estate. The most interesting of the three homes was the first one, "Toyhill," with its two interlocking cylinders and mushroom-shaped carport. In New York City the Hoffman Auto Showroom features the interior remodeling of a ground floor corner of a curtain wall skyscraper. New York City also houses the Guggenheim, one of the seventeen buildings designated to be retained by the American Institute of Architects as an example of Wright's architectural contribution to American culture. The original 1943 design, a "ziggurat," remains evident in this finalized plan. Because of the interruptions to building work caused by the Second World War, Wright had to wait thirteen years to see this project started, and it was only completed in 1959. The year the foundation stone was laid for the Guggenheim Museum (1956) also saw the construction of the "Crimson Beech," the first of the two prefabricated house designs by Wright to be constructed for the Marshal Erdman Company. While discussing New York, mention must be made of "Taliesin East" — or "Taliesin the Third" — created in the Hotel Plaza, a three-room suite which Wright remodeled for his own accommodation while overseeing the Guggenheim project.

DARWIN D. MARTIN HOUSE (1904)
125 Jewett Parkway, Buffalo
This building with its original conservatory is a large T-plan Prairie style house. It was constructed from russet Roman brick with oak trim. The glass work was by Orlando Gianinni who collaborated with Wright on many projects at this time.

W. R. HEATH HOUSE (1905)
76 Soldiers Place, Buffalo
A T-plan Prairie style house, it is primarily constructed with dark red brick. The living room opens to the south and it has a large open porch on the eastern side.

GEORGE BARTON HOUSE (1903)
118 Summit Avenue, Buffalo
Illustrated this page, opposite, and on pages 152 and 153.
This house is built to a cruciform plan with the dining room to the west, the living room east, the kitchen north and the entrance, with veranda, to the south. The house has undergone restoration. Guided tours by appointment only.

ALEXANDER DAVIDSON HOUSE (1908)
57 Tillinghast Place, Buffalo
Illustrated on pages 156 and 157.
This is built to a cruciform plan with its two-story living room facing south. It is a typical Prairie house.

DARWIN D. MARTIN GARDENER'S COTTAGE (1905)
285 Woodward Avenue, Buffalo
A house constructed from plaster on wood frame. The plans for this building were not in the Taliesin archives and it has been suggested that it was designed by one of the draftsmen in Wright's employ. (See the Martin House on page 154.)

DARWIN D. MARTIN SUMMER HOUSE AND GARAGE (1927)
"Graycliff," Lakeshore, Derby
Built close to the cliffs that drop down to Lake Erie, the structure originally had a plaster surface with wood trim but has been resurfaced. The fireplaces and chimney are of stone.

BEN REBHUHN HOUSE (1937)
9a Myrtle Avenue, Great Neck Estates
This Usonian house, with its two-story living room, was built to a cruciform plan from cypress board and batten with brickwork inside and out.

A. K. CHAHROUDI HOUSE (1951)
Petra Island, Lake Mahopac
Triangular modules are used in this single-story building. Its walls are of desert "rubblestone" with horizontal wood sheathing.

GUGGENHEIM MUSEUM (1956)
1071 Fifth Avenue at 88th Street, New York City
Illustrated on pages 151, 160 and 161.
The main gallery has a continuous spiralling inclined concrete ramp. Wright envisaged visitors taking the elevator to the top of the spiral then walking down the ramp to the ground floor. Open to the public. Guided tours by appointment only.

HOFFMAN AUTO SHOWROOM (1954)
430 Park Avenue, New York City
A concrete ramp circles around the main display floor. Some of the interior walls are surfaced with glass, as are the structural uprights of the skyscraper which houses this ground floor showroom.

EDWARD SERLIN HOUSES (1949)
12 Laurel Hill Drive, Pleasantville
USONIA HOMES The second of the Pleasantville projects is built from stone with some horizontal siding. The projected east and west extensions of Wright's original design were never built.

SOL FRIEDMAN HOUSE (1948)
11 Orchard Brook Drive, Pleasantville
USONIA HOMES The design for this house has two interlocking cylinders with a mushroom-shaped carport. Solidly constructed from stone and concrete.

ABOVE: The Davidson House. See page 154.

ROLAND REISLEY HOUSE (1951)
44 Usonia Road, Pleasantville

USONIA HOMES This single-story structure with balcony wraps around its hillside lot. Its construction is of stone with wood siding; it is the last of the Pleasantville projects.

WILLIAM CASS HOUSE (1956)
"The Crimson Beech," 48 Manor Court, Richmond

The first of the two prefabricated house designs by Wright to be constructed for the Marshal Erdman Company. This is a Marshall Erdman Company Prefab No. 1, an L-plan brick building with a masonry core and painted horizontal board and batten siding on the bedroom wing. The living room is below the entrance at the intersection of the L, and the kitchen and dining facilities, with attached carport, are in the short leg.

E. E. BOYNTON HOUSE (1908)
16 East Boulevard, Rochester

An elongated T-plan Prairie house. The building is surfaced with plaster with a wood trim. Porches at the top of the T emphasise the elongation of the plan.

MAXIMILIAN HOFFMAN HOUSE (1955)
58 Island Drive, North Manursing Island, Rye

A single-story L-plan design. It is constructed from stone, plaster and cedar shakes all trimmed with a copper fascia. The long leg of the L comprises the large living room, kitchen, and bedrooms. The short leg contains the entrance and continues on to the garage and servant's quarters. In 1972 the Taliesin Associated Architects added another wing, leading directly to the living room, providing an improved kitchen, a den, a laundry, and servant's quarters.

THIS PAGE: The Heath
House. See page 154.

OPPOSITE PAGE: The
Darwin D. Martin
Gardener's Cottage. See
page 155.

THIS and OPPOSITE
PAGE: The Solomon R.
Guggenheim Museum.
See page 155.

OHIO

The earliest example of Wright's work in Ohio was the Burton J. Westcott House in Springfield built in 1904. Of the later examples, the clerestory detailing and fascia ornamentation on the Charles E. Weltzheimer House in Oberlin is unique amongst Usonian projects. Another Usonian house, Nathan Rubin's in Canton, was originally part of a project for teachers at what is now Michigan State University. It is a mirror image of a house designed for the Usonia Homes' group in Okemos, Michigan. In Amberley Village the Gerald B. Tonkens House is a classic example of a Usonian "automatic" house, with its pierced blocks lighting the workspace. Another example of Wright's work in Ohio from 1954 is the Ellis E. Feiman House in Canton, which is based on the 1953 New York Usonian Exhibition House, now demolished; it once stood on the current site of the Guggenheim Museum. The exhibit was entitled "Sixty Years of Living Architecture" and ended up in New York after an extensive tour of Europe. There are six more examples of Wright's architecture in Ohio, all dating from the 1950s. These include the Meyers Medical Clinic in Dayton, and the last one, the Boswell House dated 1957, at Indian Hill.

GERALD B. TONKENS HOUSE (1954)
6980 Knoll Road, Amberley Village
This L-plan building, with a second L incorporating a cantilevered carport, represents a classic example of a Usonian "automatic" house. The house is constructed on a two-foot module with the standard wall block surface two feet by one foot. The wood paneling is of Philippine mahogany. The clerestory admits light through pierced blocks to the kitchen space.

JOHN J. DOBKINS HOUSE (1953)
5120 Plain Center Avenue N.E., Canton
This house is rectangular in plan and surface. It is made from brick with wood trim and a copper roof.

ELLIS A. FEIMAN HOUSE (1954)
452 Santa Clara Drive N.W., Canton
The interior space of this house is based on an L plan, with a south-facing living room opening onto a terrace. The Feimans were attracted to a Wrightian house through Alice's sister, Jeanne Rubin.

NATHAN RUBIN HOUSE (1951)
518 44th Street N.W., Canton
Constructed from brick with a horizontal wood siding sheath, the south-

east-facing bedrooms and south-facing aspect of the hexagonal living room open out onto a terrace; a pool comes off the northeast-face of the living room.

CEDRIC G. BOULTER HOUSE (1954)
1 Rawson Woods Circle, Cincinnati

Built of concrete block and Taliesin red-stained wood, this two-story house had the 1958 addition of a guest room. The second-story bedrooms jut inwards forming a gallery over the living room and outwards, making an exterior balcony to the northwest.

KENNETH L. MEYERS MEDICAL CLINIC (1956)
5441 Far Hills Avenue, Dayton

A single-story Usonian brick structure with a circular laboratory in the center of the medical section of the building. At an angle of 120° from this is the rectangular waiting room. Open to the public.

WILLIAM P. BOSWELL HOUSE (1957)
8805 Carmargo Club Drive, Indian Hill

A single-story L-plan brick structure, whose wings (west bedrooms, north services and playroom) join into the substantial living room.

KARL A. STALEY HOUSE (1950)
6363 West Lake Road, North Madison

A single-story, long I-plan house built parallel to the Lake Erie shore. It is constructed from stone, although the facade appears to have been made entirely from glass, it has so many living room windows. The house was renovated in the 1980s.

CHARLES E. WELTZHEIMER HOUSE (1948)
127 Woodhaven Drive, Oberlin

An L-plan Usonian structure using more masonry than the norm. The house has been much changed since Wright's original plan with many alterations and restoration. Guided tours available through the Allen Memorial Art Museum.

BURTON J. WESTCOTT HOUSE (1904)
1340 East High Street, Springfield

A large square-plan Prairie house, built from wood with plaster surface.

LOUIS PENFIELD HOUSE (1953)
2203 River Road, Willoughby Hills, Ohio

A two-story house constructed from concrete block and wood. The bedrooms are over the kitchen unit both adjacent to the two-story living room.

OKLAHOMA

There are three examples of Frank Lloyd Wright's architecture in Oklahoma, the earliest being a house designed for his cousin Richard Lloyd Jones in 1929. This glass and "textile-block" house — "Westhope" — has an enclosed inner courtyard with swimming pool. The other private house is that of Harold Price, Jr., the son of the Harold Price who commissioned the Price Company Tower, Oklahoma's main Wright asset. This tower, with its gold-tinted glass exterior, rises majestically out of the surrounding prairie to a height of 221 feet — nineteen stories. At the top is Mr. Price's office, complete with mural and roof garden. Listed by the A.I.A., the building passed into the hands of the Phillips Petroleum Company in 1981–82.

PRICE COMPANY TOWER (1952)
N.E. 6th Street at Dewey Avenue, Bartlesville
Illustrated above, right and on page 167.
The tower is constructed with reinforced concrete with cantilevered floors, copper louvers and copper-faced parapets. It has a gold-tinted glass exterior. Guided tours available.

ABOVE and LEFT: The
Price Tower.

HAROLD PRICE, Jr. HOUSE (1953)
"Hillside," Silver Lake Road, Bartlesville
Built to a large L-plan with a two-story living room, master bedroom and a hipped roof. An addition added a playroom to the original design.

RICHARD LLOYD JONES HOUSE (1929)
3704 South Birmingham Avenue, Tulsa
Illustrated above.
Constructed from glass and "textile-block," the building is two stories high for one third of the plan and encloses a raised inner courtyard with pool.

OREGON

The only example of Wright's work in Oregon is the T-plan Conrad E. Gordon House on the Willamette River.

RIGHT: The Price Tower.
See page 164.

CONRAD E. GORDON HOUSE (1957)
303 S.W. Gordon Lane, Wilsonville
This house is a concrete-block structure with a two-story living room. The head of the T incorporates sleeping quarters with balconies over the kitchen utilities.

P E N N S Y L V A N I A

Pennsylvania is the state which contains the best known example of Wright's houses: "Fallingwater," perched over a waterfall in the Penn highlands. Needless to say, it is one of the seventeen buildings designated to be retained by the American Institute of Architects as an example of Wright's architectural contribution to American culture. It is constructed out of reinforced-concrete slabs cantilevered out from the rock, carrying the house over the stream and waterfall on which it is built. From the square living room a suspended stairway leads directly down to the stream while, immediately above, terraces open out from the bedrooms. Wright's view of architecture was essentially romantic, poetic, and

intensely personal, and this house represents one of the most spectacular designs of his mature period. The cantilever design of "Fallingwater" is often said to have been inspired by Laura Gale's house at 6 Elizabeth Court, Oak Park.

Another fascinating Wright innovation in Pennsylania was the concept of the Suntop Homes in Ardmore. The idea was a radically different way of producing concentrated living space rather than the time-honored approach with vertically-stacked single-floor apartments. Wright's plan was to produce "quadrants" of four dwellings, with two stories per dwelling. It was intended to have four of these units built in Ardmore but in the end only one was constructed. Local protests stopped the construction of more and a further attempt to try out the idea in 1942 in Pittsfield came to nothing.

The other designs in Pennsylvania are equally interesting: there's a

ABOVE and ABOVE LEFT: The Beth Sholom Synagogue. See page 170.

a private residence at Chalkhill. The Hagan House appears to grow out of the hillside with its pointed prow resembling a ship. Then there's the remarkable Beth Sholom Synagogue in Elkins Park, another of the seventeen buildings designated to be retained by the A.I.A. The tripod-framed building was dedicated as a synagogue on September 20, 1959. Finally, in the Carnegie Museum of Art, is Wright's Field Office from San Fransisco, rebuilt as a museum exhibit. (There are other similar museum exhibits around the world — in Japan's Meija Mura museum is the rebuilt lobby of the Imperial Hotel; in the Metropolitan Museum of Art, New York there's the living room from the second Francis W. Little house; and London's Victoria and Albert Museum has on display the office of "Fallingwater" owner Edgar J. Kaufmann, Sr.)

All-in-all, Pennsylvania has a proud selection of some of Wright's finest work.

SUNTOP HOMES (1938)
152-158 Sutton Road, Ardmore

Built of brick and horizontal lapped wood siding for the Ton Company, the building is divided into four quarters, each with two stories, basement, and sunroof and each housing four families. Damage led to reconstruction which did not followed Wright's original plans.

I. N. HAGAN HOUSE (1954)
Ohiopyle Road, Chalkhill

This house employs hexagonal modules and there are no right angles at all. It is built from local sandstone, quarried at the site, and Tidewater red cypress. Tours available by appointment.

BETH SHOLOM SYNAGOGUE (1954)
Old York Road at Foxcroft, Elkins Park
Illustrated above left, right, and on page 168 and 169

Suspended from a tripod frame so that a full upper floor, directly above the chapel below, is completely free of any internal supports, the synagogue is constructed from concrete, steel, aluminium, glass, fiberglass, and oiled walnut. Guided tours by appointment only.

EDGAR J. KAUFMANN HOUSE (1935)"Fallingwater," Mill Run, State Highway 381

Wright's residential masterpiece. The guesthouse was added in 1938 and was altered in 1948. Guided tours by appointment only.

FRANK LLOYD WRIGHT FIELD OFFICE (1951)
Heinz Architectural Center, Carnegie Museum of Art, 4400 Forbes Avenue, Pittsburgh
Illustrated on page 172.

Rebuilt in the Heinz Architectural Center, this is the office Wright shared with Aaron Green in San Fransisco.

THIS PAGE: The Frank Lloyd Wright Field Office. See page 170.

SOUTH CAROLINA

There are two examples of Wright's architecture in South Carolina. The earliest is the Auldbrass Plantation in Yemassee dated 1938. The site originally contained a private residence, two cottages, a barn with chicken runs, a manager's quarters (destroyed by fire), stables with kennels, and manager's office (1939). Fire destroyed the barn and chicken runs and natural tannic acid ate through the original copper roofing. Restoration began in the mid-1980s. The other example of Wright's work in South Carolina is the private residence "Broad Margin," in Greenville. Its most obvious characteristic is the huge sheltering roof that seems to extend the hill out over the house. The living spaces of the house extend downhill from the entrance hall nestled in the hillside.

GABRIELLE AND CHARLCEY AUSTIN HOUSE (1951)
"Broad Margin," 9 West Avondale Drive, Greenville
Built into a hillside this single-story house used desert "rubblestone" and, internally, quantities of cypress. A wooden terrace was added in the 1980s off the south-facing dining area.

AULDBRASS PLANTATION (1938)
7 River Road, Yemassee, Austin
This includes the C. Leigh Stevens House, a brick and cypress construction linked to the other buildings in the complex by esplanades. Restoration of the main house and one of the cottages has been completed with many of the things not finished in the original construction correctly included straight from the plans.

TENNESSEE

This hilltop house in Chatanooga is Wright's only work in Tennessee. It's a straightforward in-line Usonian house built mainly of native Tennessee limestone.

SEAMOUR SHAVIN (1950)
334 North Crest Road, Chattanooga, Tennessee
This two-bedroom house has a living room which opens onto a north-west-facing patio. It has a "butterfly" roof.

T E X A S

The four examples of Wright's work in Texas are all from the 1950s and two stand out as being special. The first, also the earliest, is the massive single-story John Gillin House, which has floor-to-ceiling glass along its east-facing living room and grass terrace. The other notable building is the Dallas Theatre Center or, as it is known locally, the Kalita Humphreys Theater, which seats 440 people in eleven rows. Building was finished after Wright died by the Taliesin Associated Architects, as was the Sterling Kinney House. The other Wright building in Texas, the Thaxton House, fell into disrepair and was close to demolition until a sympathetic purchaser popped up in 1991 and restoration began.

STERLING KINNEY HOUSE (1957)
Tascosa Road, Amarillo
Built to a T-plan with a separate porch which forms an L around the north and west facades of a sunken living room. The main construction material is battered red brick.

WILLIAM L. THAXTON HOUSE (1954)
12024 Tall Oaks, Bunker Hill
This triangular-moduled house is built to a 60° L-plan which encloses a swimming pool. It has battered concrete-block walls.

JOHN A. GILLIN HOUSE (1950)
9400 Rockbrook Drive, Dallas
A large single-story house which completely avoids any right-angles. The main building material is stone with an unusually large amount of glass. The structure has plaster ceilings and a copper roof.

ABOVE and ABOVE LEFT: The Kalita Humphreys Theater. See page 176.

DALLAS THEATRE CENTER (1955)
3636 Turtle Creek Boulevard, Dallas, Texas
Illustrated above, above right, and on pages 174 and 175.
The design employs modules with 60° and 120° angles as well as circles.
It is a concrete cantilever construction. The circular stage drum contains
a 40-foot circular stage which itself contains a 32-foot turntable. The
foyer has subsequently been extended, and the terrace above it enclosed.
Tours by appointment only.

U T A H

The only example of Wright's work in Utah is the concrete block Stromquist House in Bountiful. The laying of the block employs a technique used in nearly all masonry work on Wright buildings; grouting in vertical joints is flush with the surface, while in the horizontal joints it is normally recessed, thus doubly emphasizing the horizontal nature of the structure.

DON M. STROMQUIST HOUSE (1958)
1151 East North Canyon Road, Bountiful
Completed by the Taliesin Associated Architects, this concrete-block structure is built on a triangular module. The triangular master bedroom and living room feature respectively a balcony and a terrace. Following deterioration under the second owner, restoration has followed.

V I R G I N I A

There are three examples of Wright's work in Virginia, all attractive Usonian houses. The Pope-Leighey House is notable for having moved location from Falls Church to Mount Vernon, although it was unsympathetically sited in its new location. Ownership and restoration are now entrusted to the National Trust for Historic Preservation. The Marden House at McClean is a hemicycle on a steep slope with views of the Potomac, but not much natural light; finally, the Cooke House is an interesting combination of a hemicycle and a parallelogram wing. It is made from imported clay from West Virginia to blend with the sand of the adjacent Crystal Lake and is topped with a copper roof.

ABOVE and LEFT: The
Pope-Leighey House.
See page 180.

LUIS MARDEN HOUSE (1952)
600 Chainbridge Road, McLean
A block and wood hemicycle that suffers from lack of light in the living room which faces west by northwest.

THE POPE-LEIGHEY HOUSE (1939))
Woodlawn Plantation, 9000 Richmond Hy, Mount Vernon
Illustrated this page, opposite, pages 178, 179, and page 182; see also Interior Design section.
A Usonian house with typical horizontal sunk cypress batten dry-wall construction around a brick core. Open March to December.

ANDREW B. COOKE HOUSE (1953)
Virginia Beach
This house is built to a plan incorporating concentric circles. The main construction materials are baked brick, made from imported clay from West Virginia, topped with a copper roof.

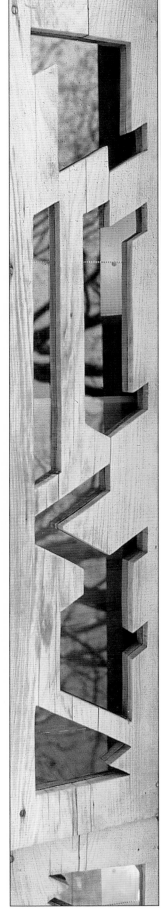

WASHINGTON

All three of Washington State's Frank Lloyd Wright buildings have concrete as their main buiding material. There's the Usonian "automatic" Tracy House, which uses perforated blocks with glass inlays between living room and terrace, and also in the clerestory; then there's the Ray Brandes House in Issaquah, which is made from concrete-block; finally, the Chauncey and Johanna Griggs House, the oldest of the three designs. Unlike the other two, this was designed to be built from stone but had to be built from concrete because of the cost of rarer materials in the immediate post-war years.

Although there are only three examples of Wright's work in Washington, his influence was felt strongly in the state, however, as architects from colleges in Illinois, who knew his work, moved into the area. Wright himself visited the region in 1931 and his impact continued as a later generation of the Taliesin Fellowship made their homes here.

RAY BRANDES HOUSE (1952)
212th Avenue at 24th Street, Issaquah
A single-story house with a central living space. Its concrete-block retaining wall is not by Wright.

W. B. TRACY HOUSE (1955)
18971 Edgecliff Drive S.W., Normandy Park
A Usonian automatic house. It employs different blocks for its inside and outside corners, walls and roof.

CHAUNCEY GRIGGS HOUSE (1946)
7800 John Dower S.W., Tacoma
This house was built to an L-plan with a two-story facade on the inside. The roofing and sidings are of cedar planks laid diagonally and horizontally giving the house the impression of a log cabin.

W I S C O N S I N

Wright was born June 8, 1867, in Richland Center, Wisconsin but it was to be 48 years before a design of his was erected there. The only work in his town of birth is the German warehouse, an imposing cube of brick and cast-in-place concrete. The top story is faced by finely patterned block and the building now houses the Richland Museum. The site of Wright's home in Wisconsin, Taliesin is the main Wrightian center in Wisconsin and, along with Oak Park and Taliesin West, is one of — if not the major — shrine to Wright. His his first design in the state, the

ABOVE: The Greek Orthodox Church, Wauwatosa. See page 194.
LEFT: The Unitarian Meeting House. See page 190.

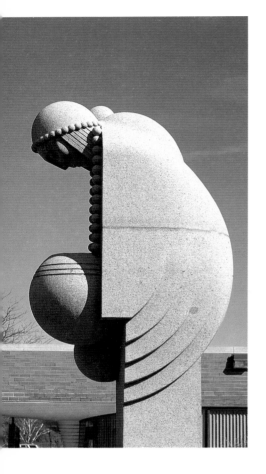

Romeo and Juliet Windmill, is there, as is his home from 1911, Taliesin itself. On the brow of a hill above the left bank of the Wisconsin River, Taliesin and the buildings in the area are a wonderful tribute to Wright and the Fellowship he set up there in 1932. They are well preserved and looked after and every enthusiast for Frank Lloyd Wright and his work should visit.

Taliesin should not, however, blind one to the other joys of Wrightian architecture in Wisconsin. The full scope of Wright's designs are illustrated well: from waterside cottages on Lake Delevan and examples of both No. 1 and No. 2 Erdman Company prefabs, through to two of his finest religious buildings, the Unitarian Meeting House at Shorewood Hills and the Annunciation Greek Orthodox Church in Wauwatosa; from two of his residential masterpieces, the last — and Wright thought the best — of the Prairie houses, "Wingspread,"and the first of the Usonians (the Herbert Jacobs First House), to his great commercial triumph, the Johnson Administration Building and Research Tower. Along with Taliesin and the Unitarian Meeting House the Johnson Building and Tower are the four listed buildings in Wisconsin.

JOSEPH MOLLICA HOUSE (1956)
1001 West Jonathan Lane, Bayside
This is an L-plan Erdman Prefab four-bedroom house and garage. Its main construction material is stone.

E. CLARKE ARNOLD HOUSE (1954)
954 Dix Street, Columbus
Originally built to a plan of two wings set at a 120° angle on a diamond module. It is built from stone. The 1959 addition by John H. Howe of Taliesin Associated Architects converted the plan to a Y.

MAURICE GREENBERG HOUSE (1954)
"Stonebroke," 3902 Highway 67, Dousman
This house is cantilevered from the brow of a hill, constructed from brick and concrete with a wood trim. Work began in stone but cash ran out and the bedroom wing was never completed.

ALBERT ADELMAN HOUSE (1948)
7111 North Barnett, Fox Point
Wright designed a laundry for Adelman in 1945: it didn't go ahead but this — and a house for Adelman's father in Arizona did. An in-line I-plan house, the garage is offset to the north accessed by a covered walkway.

RICHARD SMITH HOUSE (1950)
332 East Linden Drive, Jefferson
A single-story structure constructed from limestone, plaster, cypress and cedar shingles noted for its beautiful stonework.

GEORGE W. SPENCER HOUSE (1902)
3209 South Shore Drive, Lake Delavan

DELAVAN LAKE GROUP One of the five summer residences of the Delavan Lake Group. It is alleged that Wright disowned this cottage when the boards on the second level were laid vertically instead of horizontally during its construction.

CHARLES S. ROSS HOUSE (1902)
3211 South Shore Drive, Lake Delavan

DELVAN LAKE GROUP Originally built to a T-plan, it is a typical board and batten Prairie style house. A second-story extension — since enclosed — converted the plan to a cruciform.

FRED B. JONES HOUSE (1902)
"Penwern," 3335 South Shore Drive, Lake Delavan

DELVAN LAKE GROUP Wright built the house a gate lodge, a barn with stables, and a boathouse. The exterior is of board and batten siding while the inside features a large Roman brick fireplace. The living room has a staircase leading to a balcony which overlooks it and other rooms. It has distinctive arches on the front veranda and at the porte-cochere. This is the most extensive of the Lake Delavan Projects.

HENRY WALLIS SUMMER HOUSE (1900)
3407 South Shore Drive, Lake Delavan

DELAVAN LAKE GROUP A modest cottage similar in style to the Ward Willits House (see page 82). The horizontal board and batten siding of this cottage has generally been resurfaced.

A. P. JOHNSON HOUSE (1905)
3455 South Shore Drive, Lake Delavan

DELAVAN LAKE GROUP A symmetrical tongue-and-groove-sided Prairie style house which was extensively restored in the 1970s, retaining the original Roman brick fireplace and leaded windows.

SETH PETERSEN COTTAGE (1958)
Hastings Road off Ferndell Road, Lake Delton
Illustrated on pages 188 and 189.

This "one-room cottage" is a duplicate of the Lovness House. With views over the Mirror Lake, it is built to a square plan from native stone and wood.

PATRICK KINNEY HOUSE (1951)
474 North Filmore Street, Lancaster

This single-story house was built on triangular modules with Kinney acting as his own contractor. A stone and wood building, the northeast wing, added in 1964, is detached from the main structure.

ABOVE and LEFT:
Details from the Johnson Wax Building, Racine. See page 190.

EUGENE VAN TAMELEN HOUSE (1956)
5817 Anchorage Road, Madison

A Marshal Erdman Company No.1 Prefab, it is an L-plan brick building with a masonry core and painted horizontal board and batten siding on the bedroom wing. The Van Tamelen House featured in *House and Home* for December 1956. It is constructed from concrete block.

EUGENE A. GILMORE HOUSE (1908)
"Airplane House," 120 Ely Place, Madison

A cruciform plan with a massive sitting room, this house was substantially altered in 1928.

WALTER RUDIN HOUSE (1957)
110 Martinette Trail, Madison

A Marshal Erdman Company No. 2 Prefab, this square plan "one-room house" is built with concrete block and has painted, horizontal board and batten. A balcony outside the sleeping quarters overlooks the large two-story living room.

ROBERT M. LAMP HOUSE (1904)
22 North Butler Street , Madison

Built for an old friend, overlooking Madison's lakes, this is a simple rectangular brick Prairie house. The third story has been enclosed.

HERBERT JACOBS FIRST HOUSE (1936)
441 Toepfer Street, Madison

Considered — despite the claims of the M. E. Willey House (see page 136) — the first Usonian house. Herbert Jacobs was a reporter whose daughter would become an apprentice at Taliesin. Designed to an L-plan, the construction was typical of Usonian houses: brick and redwood.

ARNOLD JACKSON HOUSE (1957)
"Skyview," 7655 Indian Hills Trail, Beaver Dam

A Marshal Erdman Company No. 1 Prefab, this house was originally at 2909 West Beltway and moved in 1985. Original client Dr. Jackson was Wright's doctor in the 1950s. It is an L-plan brick building with a masonry core and painted horizontal board and batten siding on the bedroom wing.

HERBERT JACOBS SECOND HOUSE (1943)
7033 Old Sauk Road, Middleton

A two-story solar hemicycle with its back set into the ground (entry is via a tunnel through the wall of earth). It has a glass facade opening onto a sunken terrace.

FREDERICK C. BOGK HOUSE (1916)

2420 North Terrace Avenue, Milwaukee
Illustrated below left.
Based on a 1907 plan from *The Ladies' Home Journal* this four-square house has a terra cotta frieze under the eaves.

ARTHUR L. RICHARDS BUNGALOW (1916)
1835 South Layton Street, Milwaukee
Illustrated page 191.
Wright designed a variety of dwellings for Arthur L. Richards' companies: all were designed to be cut at the factory and shipped to the site ready for construction.

ARTHUR L. RICHARDS SMALL HOUSE (1916)
2714 West Burnham Street, Milwaukee
This single story flat-roofed house is from American System Ready-cut prefab plans of 1911.

ARTHUR L. RICHARDS DUPLEX APARTMENTS (1916)
2720-2734 West Burnham Street, Milwaukee
These four separate buildings are all from American System Ready-cut prefab plans of 1911. They each had upper and lower apartments and were originally of plaster surface and wood trim (two have since been resurfaced).

STEPHEN M. B. HUNT SECOND HOUSE (1917)
1165 Algoma Boulevard, Oshkosh
This single-story house is from American System Ready-cut prefab plans of 1911. It was landscaped by Lloyd Wright. Hunt's first house the best version of the "Fireproof House for $5,000," was at LaGrange Illinois (see page 84).

ABOVE and ABOVE LEFT: The Seth Petersen House. See page 187.

BELOW: Manona Terrace at East Martin Luther King Boulevard. A new convention center based on an interpretation of one of Wright's 1950s' designs.

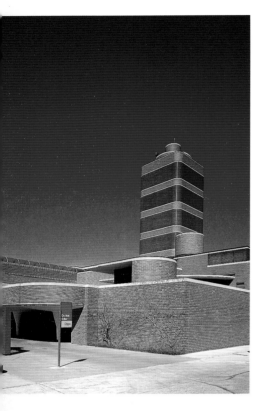

JOHNSON ADMINISTRATION BUILDING (1936) AND RESEARCH TOWER (1944)
1525 Howe Street, Racine
Illustrated left.

The Administration Building and the Tower have been designated by the A.I.A. as two of the seventeen buildings designed by Wright to be retained as supreme examples of his architectural contribution to American culture.

The main offices were completed in 1939 and have columns capable of supporting six times the weight imposed on them. Both the buildings are constructed from brick and tubular glass (not panes). The tower is totally enclosed. Guided tours available.

THOMAS P. HARDY HOUSE (1905)
1319 South Main Street, Racine

This house on Lake Michigan for the one-time mayor of Racine features a living room with an upper-story balcony and a terrace one story below street level.

KAREN JOHNSON HOUSE (1954)
1425 Valley View Drive, Racine

Karen Johnson is the daughter of the Johnson Wax owner, H. F. Johnson, whose involvement with Wright includes his home "Wingspread" (see page 194). She was married to Willard H. Keland, the first president of the corporation that built the Riverview Terrace Restaurant (see page 192). Her house saw additions in 1961 by John H. Howe.

A. D. GERMAN WAREHOUSE (1915)
300 South Church Street, Richland Center

A rectangular cube constructed from brick and cast-in-place concrete. The top story is faced by finely patterned block. This is Wright's only work in the town of his birth and the building now houses the Richland Museum. Tours by appointment only.

JOHN C. PEW HOUSE (1939)
3650 Lake Mendota Drive, Shorewood Hills

This two-story building on a hillside is constructed from limestone and cypress.

UNITARIAN MEETING HOUSE (1947)
900 University Bay Drive, Shorewood Hills

One of the seventeen buildings designated to be retained by the A.I.A. The main construction materials of the church are limestone and oak. The rising green copper roof of the church is said to symbolise hands closed in prayer. An additional wing has been added by the Taliesin Associated Architects. Guided tours available during summer months.

ABOVE RIGHT: The Richards Bungalow. See page 189.

TALIESIN
Route 23, Taliesin, Spring Green

Taliesin is the major dedicated Wrightian complex in the United States. Originally used purely to indicate Wright's house, it has come to identify the whole valley. Just off the Wisconsin River, in a valley opposite the "Welsh Hills" of Bryn Maur, Bryn Carol, and Bryn Bach, Wright rebuilt his life after the trauma of the 1909–11 period. Returning from Europe with the ex-Mrs Cheney he designed and built the first Taliesin and would go on — over half a century — to modify and build all over the area. Now preserved and run by the Frank Lloyd Wright Foundation, the Taliesin Preservation Commission oversees the buildings which encompass the complex:

1. ROMEO AND JULIET WINDMILL (1896)
Illustrated right.

The plan for the windmill reveals a diamond interlocked with an octagon. The original wood shingles were replaced with horizontal boards and battens in 1939.

2. ANDREW PORTER HOUSE (1907)

"Tanyderi" was built for Wright's sister Jane and her husband, who was head of the Hillside Home School. It is a square Prairie house. Wright, on occasion, denied that the design for this shingle-sided house was his.

3. TALIESIN (**I** 1911, **II** 1914, **III** 1925)
Illustrated pages 192 and 193.

One of the seventeen buildings designated to be retained by the A.I.A. The current Taliesin was built in 1925 after fire destroyed much of Taliesin I (1911) and II (1914). The house was constructed mainly from native limestone, wood and plaster surfacing. It has been continually altered over the years. In 1945 dams created a small lake which is used

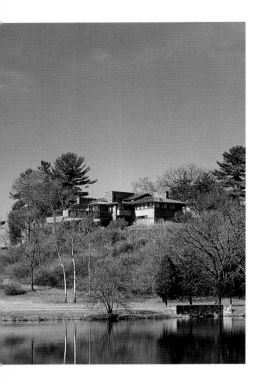

to irrigate the land as well as for recreational purposes. The garden design was Wright's last sketch. Tours available April to December.

4. TALIESIN FELLOWSHIP COMPLEX

Founded in 1933 as a school for architects, one of the first apprentices was John H. Howe, whose name crops up regularly in this book. Various buildings were created or remodelled for the Fellowship, including the Drafting Studio (1922), Playhouse (1933 and rebuilt after the fire in 1952 as the Theater), the Midway Barns (1938) and Dairy and Machine Sheds (1947), all of which helped house, feed, and nurture his community. Fellows at the Taliesin Complex ate food provided by the rich Wisconsin soil at the working agricultural estate. Later the barns and the dairy sheds provided accomodation for the expanding architectural community of Taliesin.

5. TALIESIN VISITORS' CENTER

See River View Terrace Restaurant below.

FRANK IBER (1956)
Springville Drive at U.S.5, Stevens Point

A Marshal Erdman Company No. 1 Prefab this is an L-plan brick building with a masonry core and painted horizontal board and batten siding on the bedroom wing.

RIVERVIEW TERRACE RESTAURANT (1953)
"The Spring Green," Route 23, Stevens Point, Spring Green

Now the Wright Visitors' Center at Taliesin, the restaurant was construct-

THIS PAGE and OPPO-
SITE PAGE: Taliesin.

ed for Willard H. Keland, president of the Wisconsin River Development Corp. Construction began in 1957 and was finished by the Taliesin Associated Architects after Wright's death. It utilized steel trusses obtained from the deck of the aircraft carrier *Ranger*. Building materials consist of limestone, stucco and various woods including red oak paneling.

BERNARD SCHWARTZ HOUSE (1939)
3425 Adams Sweet, Two Rivers
An early Usonian house built of red brick with horizontal cypress board and sunk batten, it overlooks the East Twin River. The building derives from Wright's idea of a home "For a Family of $5,000-$6,000 Income" as published in *Life* magazine (1938). It actually cost $18,000.

DUEY WRIGHT HOUSE (1957)
904 Grand Avenue, Wausau
Duey Wright owned a music store and the witty design of this house reflects that. Its circular living room off the main body of the house mirrors a musical note. There's a music room, four bedrooms, and views of the Wisconsin River and Rib Mountain.

CHARLES L. MANSON HOUSE (1938)
1224 Highland Park Boulevard, Wausau
The brick-built house is sheathed and partitioned by regular board and batten walls. A second-story, barely higher than the single, is accommodated by a dropped ceiling at the children's bedrooms.

ANNUNCIATION GREEK ORTHODOX CHURCH (1956)
9400 West Congress Street, Wauwatosa
The main level plan forms a Greek cross. The structure and roof form of this church is a concrete shell originally surfaced with a blue ceramic mosaic tile later replaced by a synthetic plastic resin. The truss is held by four concrete piers at the ends of the inward curving walls of the Greek cross. Guided tours by appointment only.

HERBERT F. JOHNSON HOUSE (1937)
"Wingspread," 33 East 4 Mile Road, Wind Point
This pinwheel plan, a variant of the cruciform, extends from a central three story high octagon. Wingspread is the last of the Prairie style houses to be constructed and Wright considered it to be his best and most expensive house to date.

WYOMING VALLEY GRAMMAR SCHOOL (1956)
Route 23, Wyoming Valley
This building employing 60° and 120° angles is actually a two room school with central loggia. It is constructed from concrete-block and redwood with a shingled roof. This building, with its skylighted rooms, is the only public elementary schoolhouse built from a Wright design.

LEFT and BELOW LEFT:
The German Warehouse.
See page 191.

W Y O M I N G

QUINTIN BLAIR HOUSE (1952)
Greybull Highway, Cody, Wyoming

A stone and wood house with an upward tilting living room ceiling built on the Wyoming plains east of the Yellowstone National Park. As with many of Wright's houses the porch has now been enclosed. This is the only example of his work in Wyoming.

THE INTERIOR DESIGNS OF FRANK LLOYD WRIGHT

ABOVE: Detail on pillar at Oak Park, Illinois. Frank Lloyd Wright Home and Studio 1889-1909.

RIGHT: The art glass ceiling in the dining room at Oak Park.

The unique interior designs, both of private dwellings and public spaces, of Frank Lloyd Wright can only be understood within the context of Wright's architectural philosophy, a philosophy which he expounded with characteristic vigor in his writings and lectures throughout his exceptionally long career.

In 1908 Frank Lloyd Wright published a seminal essay, "In the Cause of Architecture" in *The Architectural Record*, in which he attempted to establish his architectural philosophy. In summary, Wright stressed the importance of limiting the number of spaces to those that were necessary, and eliminating any unnecessary ornamentation and detail, a process which can be observed at work throughout the seventy years of his architectural practice, from the interior of his earliest designs such as those for his first home, Oak Park, to the interior of the Guggenheim Museum, New York.

In the interest of regarding the whole interior as an integral unit, Wright believed that necessary appliances, and indeed as much furniture as was practicable, should be built in. This process can first be observed in the early designs for his own family home and studio at Oak Park, Illinois, particularly in his extraordinary attention to detail as in the design of such features as the window seats and panelling to conceal radiators. Wright was concerned to "break the box" of the conventional room plan and achieve spatial continuity by treating wall surfaces simply and in as unbroken a manner as was feasible. Doors and other openings should be conceived as part of the integral structure. Wright desired that each home design should be unique and express the individuality of its owner, emphasising that "Simplicity and repose are the qualities that measure the true value of any work of art."

These qualities are evident in the integrated forms and colors of the interior design of the key buildings throughout his working life, beginning with Oak Park, Chicago, the house he designed in 1889 on his marriage at the age of 21. Wright believed passionately in the principle of organic architecture, although he never gave a precise definition of what he meant by the term, believing perhaps that his architecture offered its own rationale, plain for all to experience without the need for theorizing. However, some definition should be attempted for the purposes of a clearer understanding of Wright's use of organic unity in his work, a unity which extends to the design of such elements of his interior design as the furniture, fixtures and

fittings, even to the color of the upholstery, as well as the shaping of the interior space.

An understanding of Wright's concept of organic architecture is especially crucial for those in Europe, whose experience of the buildings has, of necessity, to be drawn from photographs and drawings or reconstructions of original interiors in a museum context. This lacks the excitement of experiencing the spatial and other complexities of the buildings in the original as is possible in the United States, where such key buildings as his Oak Park residence and studio are open to the public.

In *Genius and the Mobocracy*, Wright insisted that "A building can only be functional when integral with environment and so formed in the nature of materials according to purpose and method as to be a living entity." This statement contains the key to Wright's philosophy of architecture, but as with many such statements from both architects and visual artists, its meaning is easier to experience than to explain in words. Suffice it to say that organic architecture in its most readily understood form, as first articulated in Wright's early buildings, is that which is built according to natural principles, is fit for its purpose, harmonious in all its parts, with nothing that can be added and nothing taken away without detriment to the whole. This principle can be seen in Wright interiors, both public and private, from the Johnson Wax building to the Usonian houses.

Wright shared many of these ideas with his nineteenth century European predecessors, particularly with the architectural theories of William Morris and the Arts and Crafts movement in Great Britain. Wright and his predecessors shared passionate adherence to the crucial importance of the unity of form and function, the integrity of materials and the belief that the design of even humble objects was important to the whole. It was Morris who stated categorically that one should "have nothing in one's house that one does not know to be useful or believe to be beautiful," with which Wright would appear to have agreed from the design of even his early houses.

Unlike Morris however, Wright, like many of his European contemporaries, was able to defend the use of machine production, which, by the turn of the century, was more generally regarded as a positive contribution to the quality of everyday life and the means by which a hitherto undreamed of range of goods could be brought within the range of ordinary peope. An early essay by Wright, "The Art and Crafts of the Machine" (1901), was both a defence of the Arts and Crafts movement and its principles, and a critique of Morris and his followers' out-and-out hostility to machine production. Wright's use of machine production is evident from the first of his early wood interiors, and the patterned concrete design of the Ennis residence is startling and dramatic proof of Wright's embrace of machine technology.

Wright constantly revised and redefined his theories and practices throughout his long life. By the 1950s, when Wright was in his eighties, he felt the need to redefine organic architecture, in what was described

RIGHT: The studio lobby at 951 Chicgago Avenue.

RIGHT: The octagonal library of the Frank Lloyd Wright Studio at Oak Park.

FAR RIGHT: Frank Lloyd Wright's bedroom, with arched beamed ceiling.

as a lexicon of nine terms. These ranged from a redefinition of "form follows function," the rallying cry of the International Style architects whom Wright regarded as his enemies, to a term with a particular resonance for the design of Wright's interior spaces, and one that was detested by Wright's Internationalist contemporaries: "ornament" followed by "space."

For Wright "form and function" are one, while "ornament" in Wright's terminology can be compared to the expression of emotion (as in the making of poetry) which enhances the building and becomes an integrated part of the whole. The most complex of all the Wrightian definitions in *The Future of Architecture*, which was first published in 1953, was that of "space," that most crucial of the elements of architecture. At the age of eighty-six, Wright defined space as the "continual becoming, invisible fountain from which all rhythms flow to which they must pass. Beyond time or infinity. The new reality which organic architecture serves to employ in building. The breath of a work of art."

As he approached his nineties, Wright continued his emphasis on the

Fireplaces were a significant design feature in Frank Lloyd Wright's interiors, as they were in the Arts and Crafts movement.

ABOVE: Fireplace in the Wright studio.

RIGHT: The fireplace inglenook and "sacred hearth," the heart of the home at 951 Chicago avenue.

spiritual, indeed metaphysical nature of architecture. He believed that modern architecture in the 1950s lacked the essential spiritual qualities that could be conveyed by the appropriate use of such factors as space, function, ornament, and nature and thus failed to express spirituality: "Thus modern-architecture is organic-architecture deprived of a soul."

From the very beginning of his career Wright placed the plan of a building, whether it were a house-plan or one for a civic center, at the center of his architectural theory and practice. "A good plan is the beginning and the end, because every good plan is organic . . . There is more beauty in a fine ground plan than in almost any of its ultimate consequences. In itself it will have the rhythms, masses and proportions of a good decoration if it is the organic plan for an organic building with individual style — consistent with materials."

In December 1899 Wright's own house and studio, Oak Park, arguably his first "organic building with individual style consistent with materials," was presented to the public in the influential Chicago magazine *The House Beautiful*. The commentary that accompanied the photographs was by the architect Alfred H. Granger, whose praise of Wright reveals how the young architect was regarded by his contemporaries even at this early stage in his career: "I have called Mr. Wright a radical opponent of ancient styles. While he carries his opposition to antiquity to a far greater extent than many of us can agree with, it is refreshing to come into contact with a genius so fresh, so truthful and so full of vitality."

A year later in 1901 Wright published his revolutionary plans for "A Home in a Prairie Town" in the February edition of *The Ladies' Home Journal*, to be followed by a ringing declaration of his belief in modernity as he roundly rejected "the utter helplessness of old forms to satisfy new conditions" and praised the artist "who accepts, works, and sings as he works with the joy of the here and now."

Wright's rejection of old forms and his theory and practice of an "organic plan for an organic building" are very much in evidence at both his own house and studio, and in his first major commission for a large private dwelling, the Dana House, built in Springfield, Illinois in 1902 for the wealthy socialite Susan Lawrence Dana.

In 1888 Wright had married Catherine Tobin and with a loan of $5,000 the 22-year-old architect set about putting his principles into practice by designing a modest six-room bungalow for himself and his new wife in Chicago Avenue in the leafy Chicago suburb of Oak Park. A sizeable studio, containing a drafting room, an office, and a library, was later added to the house and the complex was adapted and evolved over a period of some twenty years. Oak Park became the forging ground for many of Wright's radical ideas, indeed it might be regarded as a species of laboratory in which Wright both experimented with his ideas and experienced their reality.

Wright's plan for his own house demonstrates both his early radicalism and his shared affinities with the aesthetic and moral concepts of the

THE DANA-THOMAS
HOUSE.

RIGHT: Living-hall
inglenook, looking north-
west.

contemporary British Arts and Crafts movement. This can be seen in his use of materials, particularly in the use of brick and glass, and also in the designs for furniture. It is, however, in the design of the spatial flow of the modest interior that Wright's innovatory ideas can best be appreciated. The living room is remarkable in its open plan, with a continuous string course at ceiling height emphasising the movement, continuity, and flow of the interior spaces one into another, so that the walls take on the appearance of screens: this even before Wright could have seen the Japanese Pavilion at the Columbian Exposition of 1893, which is often regarded as a pivotal point in influencing his concept of space. As Wright himself was to write later in his paper "In the cause of architecture" of March 1908, ". . .really there need be but one room, the living room with requirements otherwise sequestered from it or screened within it by means of architectural contrivances. Openings should occur as integral features of the structure and form, if possible its natural ornamentation." The door openings at Oak Park are wide and the use of oak throughout provides warmth and visual continuity as does the built-in seating. The focal point of the living room, as with so many of Wright's domestic interiors, is a brick-built "sacred hearth" within a cosy inglenook. The entire space has an intimacy and integrated flow, partially achieved, as Wright himself explained, by "lowering the ceiling surfaces and color down to the very window tops," which was to become such a feature of Wright's commissioned work.

By 1895, Frank and Catherine Tobin had four children and the domestic space at Oak Park was in obvious need of enlargement. The playroom is an exciting space, evoking ideas from Wright's own childhood learning-process with the teaching tools of Froebel's kindergarten system. This used the basic forms of nature, irreducible geometric shapes in both two and three dimensions, the so-called "gifts" provided by his mother, Anna Lloyd Wright, in her conviction that the destiny of her son was to become a great architect. Froebel's system is dependent on learning by doing, and the child learns the fundamental laws of nature by working with the simple wooden blocks and brightly colored cardboard shapes. Organic shapes drawn from nature are reduced to abstract forms in the Froebel system and the influence of this can be perceived in the design of the barrel-vaulted playroom of the newly enlarged bungalow at Oak Park, and in its detail, notably the geometric shapes of the stained glass.

The dining room of Oak Park, designed at the same time, also shows the influence of the "gifts" in its extraordinary unity of forms, particularly in its use of rectangular shapes, seen in the high-backed dining chairs and matching high-chair, but also in the wooden skylight grilles and the cell-like shapes of his designs for the windows.

The formative inspiration of Froebel's system may also be observed in Wright's early house designs on a grander scale, such as the May and the Dana-Thomas Houses, and in later years Wright was to recall his childhood inspiration in the following manner: "I sat at the little kindergarten tabletop and played . . . with the cube, the sphere and the triangle. I learned to see this way and when I did, I did not care to draw casual incidentals of Nature, I wanted to design."

Meanwhile the burgeoning architectural practice necessitated more working space and a suitably striking space in which to receive clients. Wright's studio and drafting room is an octagonally roofed two-story structure: the octagon on a cube again recalling his early childhood experience of the Froebel "gifts." Wright's radical design includes a balcony suspended on steel chains, while the top-lighting diffuses the natural light, a process aided by the characteristic art-glass panels. This lighting system is also used in the dining room, where the rectangle of the splendid dining table is echoed in the golden rectangle of the skylight above it. The stained glass of the skylight, with its curvilinear forms, is a direct evocation of the Froebel "gifts," and the integration of the irreducible geometric forms of the interior is completed by the circular shapes of the finials of the rectangular chair-backs to create one of Wright's most simple, yet satisfying, "total environments."

By the beginning of the new century, Wright was famous; famous enough to be commissioned to design an extravagant Springfield, Illinois home for the recently widowed heiress and socialite, Susan Lawrence Dana. The comparatively modest experiments with space and organic form of Oak Park are here translated into a grand and opulent mansion of thirty-five rooms. The wealth of the commission can be gauged by the fact that over four hundred and fifty specially designed stained glass panels, more than two hundred light fittings (including the famous "butterfly" pendants), and a hundred distinctive pieces of furniture were designed for the house, in addition to specially commissioned sculptures, murals, and carpets.

The Lawrence Dana house, (later to become known as the Dana-Thomas House follows its sale in 1944) like so many of the Prairie houses, focuses particularly on the design of the interior spaces. The inward-looking quality of its design and the richness of its ornament compensates for the lack of natural vegetation of its site and draws in characteristic natural forms from the locality as organic ornament. Wright designed a series of vistas, varying the ceiling heights to introduce variety, designing unexpected points of view from balconies and alcoves, and throughout shaping the space in terms of light and unified wooden panelling. Wright designed a single unifying and powerful motif for the design of the house, that of the sumac, which, together with the golden rod and purple aster (all of which, in Wright's words "characterize our roadsides in September"), forms the decorative frieze of the imposing dining room.

In *In the Cause of Architecture*, Wright explained his use of the sumac motif at the Lawrence Dana house thus, "The differentiation of a single, certain simple form characterizes the expression of one building. Quite a different form may serve for another . . . its grammar may be deduced from some plant form that has appealed to me, as certain properties in line and form of the sumach [sic] were used in the Lawrence house at Springfield." The sumac motif appears in an inventive variety of forms throughout the house, particularly in the glass panels of the dining room, the sitting room, the master bedroom and even the corridors. A variant on the sumac motif forms the magnificent metal and colored glass pendant so-called "butterfly" lamps. As with many other features of the house, the sumac motif is anticipated on the exterior by its use in the striking frieze, which embellishes and reinforces the rectilinear lines of the grand design. The house is further inextricably united with its locale by its use of the sunny colors of the fall: the gold, orange and pale yellow of the glass and the dark reddish stain of the wood.

By 1911, on his return from Europe, Wright began to plan his most famous home and working environment, Taliesin West, overlooking the Wisconsin River on his mother's land near the home of his Welsh roots. Taliesin can be translated from the Welsh as "shining brow," and Wright desired that Taliesin should be "of the hill, not on the hill." As at Oak Park, Wright remodelled the space of Taliesin over a period of time, but there the similarity ends. Taliesin was designed as a self-sufficient working community which incorporated a farm and other functional buildings stretching gradually across the hill. The complex of buildings at Taliesin West was developed over a period of forty-five years and was continuously remodelled and rebuilt after several tragic fires. It grew from the comparatively modest spaces of the original house and studio, which occupied 7,000 square feet, to the present huge complex which occupies some 37,000 square feet, without the splendid landscaped spaces of the exterior.

The interior and exterior spaces of Taliesin West were, in Wright's words, "inspired by the character and beauty of that wonderful site." The triangular motifs used throughout the complex are a direct echo of the profiles of the surrounding mountains, the buildings "of the hill, not on the hill," and an emphatic statement of Wright's organic theory of architecture. Angular and triangular shapes are used throughout the complex spaces, from the angular redwood shapes of both the form and contents of the drafting room at Taliesin, to the so-called "butterfly chairs" of the pivotal room of the living space, the garden room, which recall the paper shapes of origami.

The dominant motif of the Aline Barnsdall house, Los Angeles, is the client's favorite flower, the Hollyhock, and the house has been known as the Hollyhock House since its completion in 1917. The unifying motif can be observed throughout the house, both in its exterior and interior design, from the "art stone" (cast concrete) ornamentation of the living room fireplace, which is reflected in a shallow pool, to the design of the art glass and even the custom-designed carpets and high-backed dining chairs. Japanese screens form an important part of the design of the living room, and the integration of the room is completed by a large sofa-table with a striking wooden lamp construction, which echoes the dominant hollyhock motif of the whole concept.

The use of concrete at the Hollyhock House inspired Wright's infinitely more complex fashioning of this supremely flexible material, whose

LEFT: The drafting room at Taliesin West, showing the angular redwood forms of the roof, now covered with plastic.

BELOW: View of the Hollyhock House living room, showing the hearth and the recreated sofa-table with its integrated hollyhock motif lamp.

THE ENNIS BROWN
HOUSE.

RIGHT (DETAIL) and FAR
RIGHT: Stacked textile
concrete blocks form a
colonnade, through
which can be seen the
hearth with the Tiffany
"wisteria" mosaic.

uses had even been exploited by the Romans. Wright had begun his exploration of concrete's malleability in his design for Unity Temple in Oak Park in 1904. At the monumental Ennis House in Los Angeles of 1923, Wright used a form of stacked textile-patterned concrete blocks, with forms reminiscent of Mayan designs. For the splendid colonnade, which links the indoor and outdoor spaces, Wright offset the geometry of the stacked cubic forms of the columns by the curving forms of wisteria in the golden glass Tiffany mosaic above the hearth. Used as a continuing motif, the forms of the sumptuous wisteria mosaic are made to assume abstract form in the last art glass of this kind that Wright was to design.

Wright, the quintessential American architect, was a man very much in touch with his time, never less so than in his invention of the Usonian house during the Depression years as a solution to the problem of low-cost housing for middle-income families. The derivation of the term "Usonian" is mysterious, but undoubtedly derives from "USA," not the contemporary United States of America which Wright, now in his seventies, perceived about him, but more a utopian ideal of the future. (The term first comes to attention in a 1925 article entitled "In the Cause of Architecture: The Third Dimension" and Wright would expand on it though his writings.) As ever, however modest the building, Wright wanted to integrate the structure and the site, and this is a marked feature of the various types of Usonian homes, however different. In his extraordinary ability to adapt to changing social and economic needs, however, the Usonian concept differs radically from previous types of Wright homes. This is nowhere more apparent than in their plan and in the organization of interior space, which reflects Wright's response to the seismic changes in family life since the architect's designs for his own home at Oak Park in the 1890s, and particularly to the changing status of women. As Wright himself explained, in the modern, servantless household, the woman of the house became the central figure, a "hostess 'officio' [instead of] . . . a kitchen mechanic behind closed doors." The kitchen itself was moved to the center of the house and renamed a "work space" from which the woman of the house could supervize everything: "family processes are conveniently centralized" was his commentary in 1948 of a Usonian design of a decade before, so that "the mistress of the house can turn a pancake with one hand while chucking the baby into a bath with the other." The change can also be seen to reflect the new informality of domestic life, particularly with regard to meals and their serving, whether family meals or entertaining guests. The formal dining room, which had once been regarded as a separate, dedicated space, had lost its function and become an anachronism. This process can be seen at work in the organization of the interior space of such Usonian houses as the Zimmerman House, the Loveness House and the Rosenbaum and Walter Houses, as well as the Pope-Leighey House, where the Usonian idea can be seen perhaps at its simplest and most functionally efficient.

Loren Pope, a newspaperman, requested a house from Wright for a site

ABOVE: The Usonian Zimmerman House, Manchester, New Hampshire, 1950. The garden room originally doubled as a concert room. The Zimmermans loved music and the quartet stand and stools are based on Wright's designs for Taliesin.

LEFT: The Walter House at Cedar Rock, Quasqueton, Iowa, 1944. The living or garden room, give extensive views of the Wapsipinicon River. The pierced roof and huge windows allow enough light to sustain a flourishing interior garden.

THE POPE-LEIGHEY
HOUSE.

RIGHT: The living area
showing the modular
plywood seating, which
can be moved into a
variety of configurations
depending on the
occasion.

LEFT: Another view of the Zimmermans' living room.

FAR LEFT: View of the Johnson Wax Company's Main Office, (the "Great Workroom") showing Wright's total working environment in its most homogenous form, with its dramatic top-lit light source and inward-looking design.

in Falls Church, Virginia, and Wright complied with such an efficient and flexible design of wood, brick, and glass mounted on a concrete pad that, when in 1964 the house was threatened by a planned interstate highway, the whole structure could be removed and rebuilt at the National Trust-owned Woodlawn Plantation, in Mount Vernon, Virginia.

The interior space of the living area at this house, as with other Usonians, is designed for maximum flexibility, with modular — in this case easily moved plywood — furniture and comfortable seating. Another characteristic of Usonian houses can be observed particularly clearly both here and at the later Zimmerman House in Manchester, New Hampshire of 1950. This is in the fenestration or lighting of the interior, which in both houses has windows at a high or clerestory level to permit changing views of the trees outside. At the Zimmerman House, Wright responded to his clients' need for a living area that was also to double as a concert space by designing a space in which all other rooms are relatively small in size, subsidiary to the living, or garden, room which opens onto a terrace and landscaped garden beyond. The relatively modest scale of the house is

JOHNSON WAX
COMPANY
ADMINISTRATIVE
OFFICES.

ABOVE: The curvilinear
forms of the interior are
echoed in the integrated
design of the elegant
office furniture. The
chairs have pivotal backs
and the desk drawers
may also be
pivoted.

RIGHT: The imposing
entrance atrium.

spatially expanded by the use of materials, and an imaginative organic integration of the house and its setting which recalls the earlier Prairie houses — proof, if proof were needed, of Wright's continuing powers in a career which by this time had spanned seven decades.

In another garden room, at the Walter House at Quasqueton, Iowa, on a hill overlooking the Wapsipinicon River, Wright responded to the spectacular site by adding a pierced roof to huge main windows which, with the addition of clerestory windows, flood the interior with light enough to sustain an interior garden.

Wright's abiding principle of organic-architecture was applied equally, and indeed simultaneously, to the design of both public and private buildings throughout his career, from the Larkin Company Administrative Building in Buffalo of 1902–06 to the Solomon R. Guggenheim Museum, New York, which was begun in 1943 and not completed in its original form until 1959, the year of Wright's death. Indeed one of Wright's most important clients, the Pennsylvanian department store owner Edgar J. Kaufmann, was to commission the architect for both his private domain at Fallingwater and public working environment in the luxuriously appointed Kaufmann Office, which, since its reinstallation at the Victoria and Albert Museum, London in 1993, is the only complete Frank Lloyd Wright interior on public display in Europe.

The Kaufmann Office, which was designed in 1935-37, although elaborate and luxurious in its detail, was relatively modest in size and bore little relation to the surrounding spaces of Kaufmann's department store in which it was housed. Before the Second World War, Wright's most important design for a total working environment was undoubtedly that of the Johnson Wax Company's headquarters at Racine, Wisconsin, which was under construction 1936–39. Of all the interior spaces, it is the main office, which rises two stories in height, which is undoubtedly the most spectacular. As with Wright's domestic interiors, it demonstrates Wright's radical concepts of plasticity and continuity. Indeed organic-architecture in Wright's philosophy can here be demonstrated to such a degree that the Johnson Wax building may well be regarded as the quintessential Wrightian example of the total environment in the public domain. In the fluid space of the main office, the cone-like columns support the circular modules of the roof deck to form an integrated total environment which is dramatically enhanced by the use of top lighting. The light is diffused through a series of glass tubes, which creates an extraordinary sense of internalized light, all of a piece with the inward-looking design of the building as a whole. The almost hermetic environment reflects Wright's long-held belief in the nature of work as essentially sacred, requiring complete concentration, free of any distraction. Similar symbolic use of inward looking working space may be seen in the Kaufmann Office.

The complete integration of the interior spaces of the building is enhanced by the furniture designed for the building, also conceived in

ABOVE: The Price Company Headquarters Tower. Mr. Price's office with built-in furniture and signed mural.

RIGHT: Auditorium at the Dallas Theatre, also known as the Kalita Humphreys Memorial Theater, built in 1959.

circular modules and organically related to the building's interior so that each part of the design becomes an integrated and inseperable part of the whole. The spare and elegant office chairs and tables have unusual design features, not least the pivoting chair backs and the storage drawers which may also be pivoted. The functionality and ingenuity of the design is enhanced by the red coloration of even the most humble typist's chair, an aesthetic consideration which adds a typically Wrightian warmth to the interiors throughout the building and is very unusual in a working environment.

Wright himself was aware of his achievment in the Johnson Wax building, writing in his autobiography ". . . let's say here that it is technically and in the entire realm of the scientific art of Architecture, one of the world's most remarkable structures. I like it. They like it. Let it go at that."

Post-war, Wright's major office development is generally considered to be the H. C. Price Tower at Bartlesville, Oklahoma. Developed from designs originally conceived in the 1920s, Price Tower combines office suites and apartments on each of its 16 stories. The differentiation between home and work environments is marked externally by the use of vertical louvers for the residential areas and horizontal for the working spaces, while internally the sharp angular forms of the fixtures and fittings are analagous in design to the crimped metal detail of the curtain walls of the entire structure. Particularly striking features of Wright's design are the metal "dentist-type" upholstered chairs throughout the building and Mr. Price's own office and apartment at the very top of the building, with its striking mural of angular forms and wooden variants of what might be termed the Price Tower chair. The design throughout in its spiky angularity is in striking contrast to the curving spatial flow of the Johnson Wax building.

In later life Wright was to receive commissions for various forms of auditoria the length and breadth of America, from the Kansas City Community Christian Church to the Beth Shalom Synagogue, Pennsylvania, and the Dallas Theatre Center of 1959. As early as 1920 Wright had begun to formulate ideas for auditoria, based on projects when he was in training with Sullivan and Adler. He continuously modified these ideas into what he termed a "New Theatre," and after an unusually lengthy gestation period his ideas finally reached concrete form in 1959 in the Kalita Humphreys Memorial Theatre. The theatre reverses the conventional disposition of space: the seating and the revolving stage (which is some forty feet in diameter) are conceived as a unity rather than separate spaces, and the radical reshaping of the theatrical space, together with the extensive underground workshop and scenery-storage facilities, make greater communication and control possible.

In the last five years of his life, Wright was to design five religious buildings, which include the Kansas City Church and the Beth Sholem Synagogue, in Philadelphia. At the Beth Sholem Synagogue, the structure is conceived as a huge, translucent, pyramid-like form, roofed in glass

THE BETH SHOLEM
SYNAGOGUE.

RIGHT: Interior view.
The translucent,
pyramidal shape of the
synagogue is very char-
acteristic of Wright's daring approach to such
commissions: he
designed no fewer than
five religious buildings in
the last years of his life.

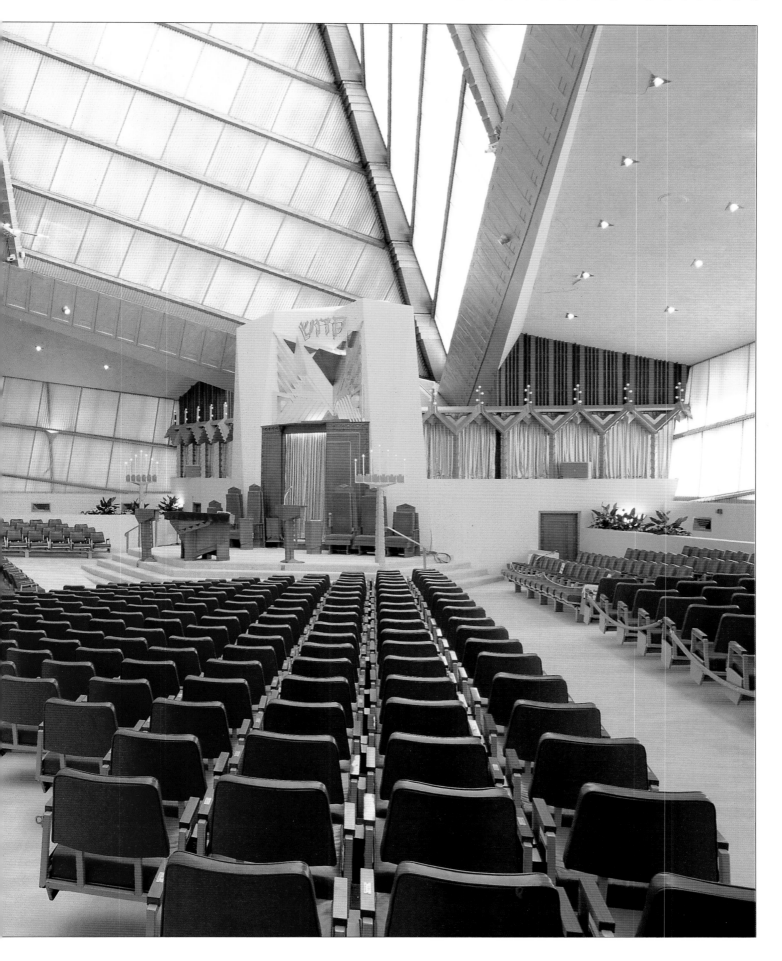

RIGHT: Interior view of auditorium of the Southern College, Lakeland, Florida.

BELOW: Guggenheim Museum — The transparent dome which spans the entire vast central space.

and corrugated plastic sheeting. Internally the basic triangular forms of the ground plan and the structure are repeated in the triangular design module of such elements as the stained glass and other fixtures.

The huge complex of Florida Southern College, Lakeland, which started building in 1940 and remained unfinished on Wright's death, contains many characteristically Wrightian elements, especially in the design of the chapel, which, because of the absence of an altar, is reminiscent of Wright's auditoria designs, particularly in its top lighting. The College designs for the entire campus which were designed to include a library, laboratories, lecture rooms, an outdoor theatre and extensive faculty buildings, was Wright's most comprehensive work even in its uncompleted state, exceeded only in size by the Marin County Civic Center at San Rafael, California. Wright had hardly finished the designs for the huge domed auditorium and long enclosures housing administrative offices before his death in April 1959. The building, which was begun in 1962 by the Taliesin Fellowship, must be regarded as posthumous, although various Wrightian hallmarks are clear, particularly in the use of top-lighting and the spherical and hemispherical cut-out designs of the roofing structures.

The Solomon R. Guggenheim Museum of 1959 as it now appears must also be regarded as posthumous. The bizarre external shape of the building, and the difficulties of hanging large works of art within it, do nothing to lessen its internal impact. The great spiral ramp takes the visitor five complete turns from top to bottom, determining the view of both building and contents to an extraordinary degree. Additional light to that given by the translucent spaces between the spirals of the ramp is characteristically provided by a vast central dome. Wright's final, astonishing total environment proves, if proof were needed, that the great architect had lost none of his vision and daring at the age of 92.

ABOVE: Frank Lloyd
Wright Home and Studio
1889-1909. Living-room
bay, looking southeast.

THE DANA-THOMAS
HOUSE.

RIGHT: Dining-room
and vault, looking south.

FAR RIGHT: Master
bedroom, looking
predominantly north.

THE DANA-THOMAS
HOUSE.

RIGHT: Wall fountain in
entrance hallway "The
Moon Children," by
Richard Bock, with art
glass screens with sumac
motifs.

BELOW and BELOW
RIGHT: Front and rear
views of "Flower in
the Crannied Wall"
sculpture by Richard
Bock.

FAR RIGHT: "Butterfly"
pendant lamp from the
dining room.

THE DANA-THOMAS
HOUSE.

RIGHT and FAR RIGHT:
Art-glass screens and
windows with sumac
and rectilinear motifs.

230

TALIESIN WEST.

ABOVE: The Garden Room, social hub of the house.

RIGHT: The battered rubble walls and hearth of the Garden Room.

FAR RIGHT: The triangular motifs of the garden room are repeated in the "butterfly" chairs, reminiscent of folded origami.

THE ALINE BARNSDALL
HOLLYHOCK HOUSE.

RIGHT: The living room
fireplace, which is
reflected in a shallow
pool.

BELOW RIGHT: The
dining room with its
distinctive hollyhock
motif chairbacks.

FAR RIGHT: Integrated
hollyhock motif in
the design of a concrete
pillar.

THE ALINE BARNSDALL
HOLLYHOCK HOUSE.

RIGHT: The specially
designed hollyhock motif
carpet.

236

THE ENNIS BROWN HOUSE.

ABOVE: Dining area with the stacked textile blocks, whose distinctive motifs are reminiscent of Mayan designs, with a vista of the colonnade beyond.

RIGHT: View from the hearth area to the colonnade and "outdoor rooms" beyond.

FAR RIGHT: Corridor leading off the entry hall.

RIGHT: Another view of the Pope-Leighey House: the living area, showing the flexible seating and the high, plywood cut-out window panels, so characteristic of Usonian houses.

BELOW RIGHT: The garden room of the Walter House.

OPPOSITE ABOVE: The Stanley and Mildred Rosenbaum House in Florence, Alabama, designed in 1939. The living area opens off to the dining area and the kitchen. The cypress built-in furniture was specially designed for the room by Wright.

OPPOSITE BELOW: The Rosenbaum's dining area, with the entrance to the kitchen on the left. The plywood dining chairs are by Charles Eames.

PRICE COMPANY
HEADQUARTERS
TOWER.

RIGHT: Office and
integrated furniture. The
design of the so-called
"dentist" chair (here
in metal), which is so
characteristic of the
sharply angular modules
of Price Tower's total
environment is in
striking contrast to the
design concept of the
Johnson Wax Building.

BELOW RIGHT: External
view of the Price Tower.

FAR RIGHT: Globe in
Price's office.

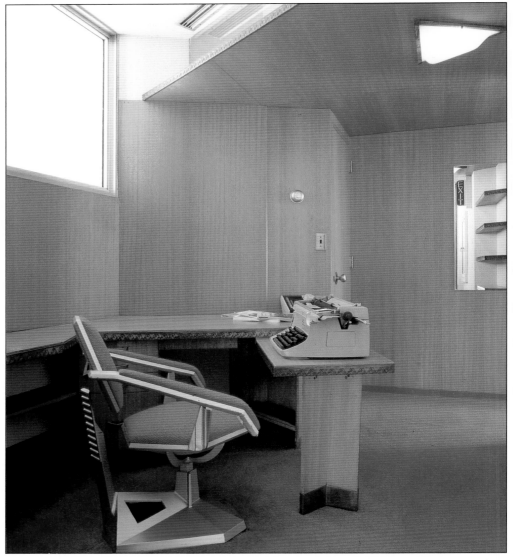

242

THIS PAGE and OPPOSITE: The Southern College, Lakeland, Florida.

244

D E M O L I S H E D
B U I L D I N G S

ARIZONA

Ocatillo Desert Camp, Chandler (1928)

A temporary encampment established by Wright while working on the San Marcos-in-the-Desert project for Dr. Alexander Chandler. (See Introduction.) The result was so successful that it became the prototype for Taliesin West.

COLORADO

Horseshoe Inn, Estes Park (1908)

No documentation remains on this building, but it probably resembled the Como Orchard Summer Colony project (University Heights, Bunkhouse Road, Darby, Montana). Built for Willard Ashton.

ILLINOIS

Browne's Bookstore, Chicago (1908)

Wright designed the interior details as well as the building.

Francis Apartments, Chicago (1895)

Built for the Terre Haute Trust Company, the ground floor of this four-story building was surfaced in the style of Sullivan with a geometrical pattern. The north wing on the ground floor contained four shops.

Francisco Terrace Apartments, Chicago (1895)

Illustration: *Above right.*
This was a two-story brick complex intended as good quality but cheap housing. It was one of the two sets of apartments built for Edward C. Waller, a neighbor of Wright's friend William H. Winslow. General neglect led to vandalism and eventual demolition although the entry archway was reconstructed at Euclid Place, Oak Park in 1977.

Edward C. Waller Apartments, Chicago (1895)

These were better quality apartments than those of Francisco Terrace.

Allison Harlan House, Chicago (1892)

Of the many "bootleg" projects, this was probably the one that led to Wright's split from Adler & Sullivan.

L. K. Horner House, Chicago (1908)

Very similar in plan to Mrs. Thomas Gale's residence in at 6 Elizabeth Court, Oak Park.

Joseph Husser House, Chicago (1899)

Forerunner of the Prairie house and a notable loss. As with the Prairie houses, with their living quarters above ground level, this building had the basement at ground level with the house rising two stories higher — as much as anything for protection from flooding by nearby Lake Michigan. The furniture designed by Wright was saved and the dining room (complete with table and chairs) was auctioned in 1987 making $1.6 million.

W. S. McHarg House, Chicago (1891)

This house was the first of Wright's nine "bootlegged" designs created while he was working for Adler & Sullivan.

Midway Gardens, Chicago (1913)

Conceived by Edward C. Waller Jr, this huge restaurant-cum-entertainment complex occupied an entire city block. It was notable for its patterned concrete blocks and brick work. In the end it ran for two years before being sold to a Chicago brewer who was put out of business by prohibition.

Mori Oriental Art Studio, Chicago (1914)

Wright decorated the interior of a corner room on the eighth floor of the Fine Arts Building on Michigan Avenue for use as an art studio.

Oscar Steffens House, Chicago (1909)

Situated near Lake Michigan, the Oscar Steffens House had the typical two-story living room of the Prairie style houses.

RIGHT: The Francisco Terrace entry archway at Euclid Place, Oak Park.

Peter C. Stohr Arcade Building, Chicago (1909)

Most of this building was located under the "El" tracks at Wilson Avenue Station. The building incorporated the stairs to the railway and ticket booths and rose to three stories where it was free of the tracks.

Albert Sullivan House, Chicago (1892)

Louis Sullivan lived in the house for four years before his brother occupied the premises. Wright designed it while working for Sullivan in the style of his "*Lieber Meister.*"

Thurber Art Gallery, Chicago (1909)

As with Pebbles & Balch Shop and Browne's Bookstore, Wright took great care over the interior spaces. Two long panels of leaded glass lit the gallery on sunny days concealing the otherwise indirect lighting.

Fox River Country Club, Geneva (1907)
Destroyed by fire: c. 1910

The existing Country Club belonging to Colonel George Fabyan on his private land was remodeled by FLW to bring it up to contemporary standards. Like the Game Preserve remodeling (1511 Batvia Road, Geneva) it was a reworking of an existing structure.

Grace Fuller House, Glencoe (1906)

A small house, this was the second and much more modest of the two Prairie houses designed by Wright in Glencoe.

Herbert Angster House, Lake Bluff (1911)

Hidden in dense woodland in ideal natural fashion, this was a plaster-surfaced, wood-trimmed Prairie house.

H.W. Bassett House Remodeling, Oak Park (1894)

No contemporary records appear to have been made of this building, so nothing is known about its appearence or the alterations made by Wright.

Pebbles & Balch Shop, Oak Park (1907)
The interior and exterior of this building exhibited the influences of Wright's visit to Japan. The interior used natural woods and oiled paper for glass.

Park Ridge Country Club Remodeling, Park Ridge (1912)

The country club was both altered and added to by Wright.

E.W. Cummings Real Estate Office, River Forest (1905)

This building was a Prairie structure of wood and plaster with broad overhanging eaves, partially hidden by a large curtain wall.

River Forest Golf Club, River Forest (1898)

A T-plan, single-story, board and batten construction with a 1901 addition.

Edward C. Waller House Remodeling, River Forest (1899)

The remodeling of this large house in Auvergne Place included the dining room and other interior work. The separate stables were also demolished.

MICHIGAN

Walter Gerts Cottage, Whitehall (1902)

The original plan for this house was a rectangular, single-story board and batten structure with a centrally located fireplace.

MINNESOTA

Francis W. Little Residence II, Deephaven (1912)

"Northome" had Wright's most spacious interior at that time of his Prairie period with its 55-foot living room. At the time of the building's demolition, various museums removed sections for later reconstruction. The living room was reconstructed at the Metropolitan Museum of Art (New York City) while the library was reconstructed at the Allentown Art Museum (Pennsylvania). This was Wright's first building in Minnesota.

MISSISSIPPI

Welbie L. Fuller House, Pass Christian (1951)

With its exposed natural concrete block and rough-sawn yellow pine this house was in many ways unique among Wright's late works. It fell in the face of the tidal wave caused by Hurricane Camille.

MONTANA

Como Orchard Summer Colony, University Heights, Darby (1908)

A small land office and one altered cottage are all that remain from this project.

Bitter Root Inn, Stevensville (1908)

The inn was originally intended to be part of the Bitter Root Irrigation District. Houses in the area show Prairie school influences although none of them have been specifically attributed to any of the major Chicago architects of the time.

NEW YORK

Larkin Company Administration Building, Buffalo (1903)

Wright got this job through his friendship with William E. Martin, from Oak Park, whose brother, Darwin D. Martin, worked with Larkin. Notable for its monolithic structure and large atrium, the Larkin building used plate glass and air conditioning — a first in commercial buildings. The austere exterior was enlivened by sculpture by Wright's regular collaborator, Richard Bock.

Buffalo Exposition Pavilion, Buffalo (1901)

No plans or photographs seem to have survived this work or that in Madison Square Garden, New York City (see below). Both were commissioned by the Universal Portland Cement Company.

New York City Exhibition (1910)

See above.

Hotel Plaza Apartment Remodeling, New York (1954)

Wright remodeled an apartment in the Hotel Plaza to use as temporary accommodation while working on the Guggenheim Museum and his other projects in New York and Connecticut. It was known to some as "Taliesin the Third" or "Taliesin East."

PENNSYLVANIA

Edgar J. Kaufmann Sr. Office, Pittsburgh (1937)

This office for the Kaufmann Department Store was reassembled in the Victoria and Albert Musuem, London. Wright's chairs and other furniture are complemented in the museum display by a cypress plywood mural in relief.

RIGHT: The last remaining wall of the Larkin Administrative building under snow in New York.

WISCONSIN

Geneva Inn, Lake Geneva (1911)

This Prairie-style structure commissioned by Arthur L. Richards was of wood frame and the main lobby featured a large Roman brick fireplace.

Robert M. Lamp House, Governor's Island, Lake Mendota (1893)

Though living in Oak Park at the time, Wright maintained contact with the area around Madison, his birthplace. This house was built for a boyhood friend.

Municipal Boathouse, Madison (1893)

Wright won a Madison Improvement Association competition for design of the boathouse. Its large, lake facing arch was to be featured in later Wright designs.

Arthur Munkwitz Duplex Apartments, Milwaukee (1916)

These buildings were the result of Wright's designs for his American System Ready-Cut structures with their pre-fabricated construction essential to the concept. These buildings were based on the American Model A4 home. Two Model A4 units were built, one above the other to form a duplex. The term "quadraplex" comes from the joining of two of these duplexes with a common entryway.

Hillside Home School I, Spring Green (1887)

Wright's aunts Nell and Jane Lloyd Jones taught in this school for many years. In 1903, a larger structure was built. With much restructuring it eventually became part of the Taliesin Fellowship complex. See page 192.

Taliesin I, Spring Green (1911)

See Introduction.

Taliesin II, Spring Green (1914)

See Introduction.

JAPAN

Imperial Hotel, Tokyo (1915–22)

A huge job which saw Wright involved in meticulous detail — even including the design of carpets — the hotel was so well designed and constructed that it withstood the major earthquake of 1923. On demolition the entrance lobby was was moved to Nagoya.

CHRONOLOGY

1866	William Cary Wright, itinerant music teacher and Baptist minister, marries Anna Lloyd Jones, his second wife.
1867	June 8, Frank Lloyd Wright born in the Richland Centre, Wisconsin.
1874	William Cary Wright returns to New England to become parson in Weymouth, Massachusetts.
1876	Visits the Centennial Exposition and FLW's mother discovers Froebel's "toys."
1877	The family moves to the state capital: Madison, Wisconsin.
1884	FLW's parents separate and his father leaves. Father and son become estranged.
1885	FLW apprenticed to the only professional builder in the area, Allen D. Connover, also the Dean of Engineering at the University of Wisconsin.
1887	FLW leaves for Chicago: finds employment with Joseph Silsbee. In the fall gets a job as draftsman with the prestigious firm of Adler and Sullivan.
1888	Marriage to Catherine Lee Tobin, daughter of a Chicago businessman. Begins building his home and studio at Oak Park, Illinois. This is the oldest building designed by the architect still in existence.
1889	Signs five-year contract with Adler & Sullivan.
1893	The World's Fair opens in Chicago. "Bootlegged" houses for Oak Park. Leaves Adler & Sullivan and sets up in independent practice in Steinway Hall, Chicago. First independent project is the William H. Winslow House.
1894	Writes his first essay on architecture.
1895	Builds a studio adjacent to his house at Oak Park. FLW opens his own office in Chicago.
1899	Joseph Husser House, overlooking Lake Michigan, designed — the precursor of the Prairie house style.
1900	First Prairie Houses built for Harley Bradley and Warren Hickox on adjacent lots in Kankakee, Illinois.
1901	Contributes several model house designs for publication in *The Ladies' Home Journal*, including "A Home in a Prairie Town" and "A Small House with 'Lots of Rooms in It'." Ward W. Willits House designed — certainly one of the finest Prairie Houses. Frank Wright Thomas House, the first Prairie-style house FLW designed and built in Oak Park.

1903   Larkin Building designed.

1905   First visit to Japan; buys considerable amount of Japanese art.

1906   Frederick C. Robie House designed — probably the best known of the Prairie Houses.

1908   Collaborates with Frederick Gookin to present a collection of Hiroshige prints at Chicago's Institute of Art.

1909   Shuts down Oak Park studio, leaves his wife and six children, and departs for Europe with Mamah Borthwick Cheney. Collaborates with the German publisher Ernst Wasmuth in producing a mongraph of his works. Initially lives in Berlin, then moves near Florence.

1910   Publication of the Wasmuth monograph, *Ausgeführte Bauten und Entwürfe von Frank Lloyd Wright.*

1911   Returns to the USA with Mrs. Cheney. Begins building Taliesin I in Spring Green, Wisconsin.

1913   To Japan with Mamah Cheney to secure the Imperial Hotel Commission.

1914   Gets Imperial Hotel commission. Murder of Mrs. Cheney and her children, plus four others at Taliesin I. Taliesin I gutted by the subsequent fire.

1915   FLW sails for Japan, with the sculptress Miriam Noel. Accepts the commission to design and build the new Imperial Hotel, Tokyo.

1916   FLW and Miriam move to Tokyo for the building of the Imperial Hotel.

1917   The Hollyhock House designed.

1922   Return full-time to the USA. Catherine agrees to a divorce so Wright free to marry Miriam; they separate after six months.

1923   "La Miniatura," the first Textile Block House, designed for Alice Madison Millard.

1924   Sullivan dies and FLW writes his obituary. Meets Olgivanna Milanov née Lazovich Hinzenberg, his third and final wife. Olgivanna moves in to join FLW at Taliesin II.

1925   FLW and Olgivanna's daughter Iovanna is born. The living quarters at Taliesin II burn down during an electrical storm.

1926   FLW and Olgivanna move anonymously to a cottage in Minneapolis for the summer. Around this time starts writing his autobiography.

1927   Arizona Biltmore Hotel designed.
        FLW auctions a number of his Japanese prints in New York to raise money to relieve his huge debts. The bank repossesses Taliesin and his art collections. Family moves for a time to New York to live with sister Maginel.

1928   On August 25 FLW and Olgivanna marry. Move to Arizona for the San Marcos-in-the-Desert project. Frank Lloyd Wright Inc. is established to finance him, so is able to move back to Taliesin.

1929   Stock market crash and the start of the Depression. Many projects are cancelled as a direct result. FLW establishes Ocatillo Camp, in Arizona.

1931   FLW lectures at Princetown University, also published as *Modern Architecture*. "Two Lectures on Architecture" published by the Art Institute of Chicago.

1932   *An Autobiography*, the first edition of FLW's memoirs, is published.
The Taliesin Fellowship founded at Spring Green.

1933   Malcom E. Willey House designed — considered to be the major link between the Prairie and Usonian designs.

1935   Broadacre City model prepared for the Industrial Arts Exhibition at the Rockerfeller Center.

1936   First Usonian houses designed, notably the Herbert Jacobs House and Fallingwater — many people would call the latter his masterpiece.

1937   Starts to build Taliesin West at Scottsdale, Arizona.
Visits Soviet Russia but is unimpressed with the architecture.

1940–42 Writes 10 pacifist anti-intervention essays. Alienates many former friends.

1943   Duell, Sloan and Pearce published his revised *An Autobiography*. In June is approached to design the Guggenheim Museum, meets Solomon R. Guggenheim and signs the contract. Gets a two-room apartment at the Plaza Hotel, New York from which to supervize the project.
The Second Jacobs House designed — the first "solar hemicycle."

1949   November, Guggenheim dies and the musuem is in jeopardy.

1950   Senator McCarthy tries to impeach Wright as an anti-American Communist.

1952   Harold C. Price Company Tower designed.
The Pieper House, the first Usonian "Automatic" house, built.

1954   Beth Sholom Synagogue, Elkins Park, Pennsylvania.
The Natural House published by Horizon Press, in which FLW defines the Usonian concepts of moderate price, natural materials, prefabrication, slab roofs, and versitilty of design to suit the particular site and client.

1956   Annunciation Greek Orthodox Church, Wauwatosa, Wisconsin.
Solomon R. Guggenheim Museum, New York.

1957   Marin County Civic Centre, San Rafael, California begun. It was not finished until after FLW's death.

1958   *The Living City* published.

1959   FLW dies, after an illustrious career spanning almost 75 years. Is buried at Taliesin North in the family plot next to Mamah Cheney.

1985   His body is disinterred and taken to Taliesin West where his ashes are mingled and buried with Olgivanna's.

RIGHT: The Frank Lloyd
Wright Home and
Studio, 951 Chicago
Avenue, Oak Park.

BELOW: Taliesin West,
California.

INDEX

ABLIN HOUSE, California 34, *34, 35,* 36

ABRAHAM LINCOLN CENTER, Illinois 70, 76, *76*

ADAMS (HARRY S.) HOUSE, Illinois 85, *85*

ADAMS (JESSIE) HOUSE, Illinois 77, *77*

ADAMS (MARY M.W.) HOUSE, Illinois 82, *108*

ADELMAN (BENJAMIN) HOUSE, Arizona 24

ADELMAN (ALBERT) HOUSE, Wisconsin 186

AFFLECK HOUSE, Michigan 128

"AIRPLANE HOUSE" (GILMORE HOUSE), Wisconsin 188

ALLEN HOUSE, Kansas 120, *122–123,* 123, *124, 125*

ALPAUGH STUDIO, Michigan 132

ALSOP HOUSE, Iowa 116

AMBERG HOUSE, Michigan *127,* 130

ANDERTON COURT SHOPS, California 34, 36–38, *36, 37*

ANGSTER HOUSE, Illinois 247

ANNUNCIATION GREEK ORTHODOX CHURCH, Wisconsin *184–185,* 186, 194

ANTHONY HOUSE, Michigan 128, *129*

ARIZONA BILTMORE HOTEL *14,* 14, 20, *22,* 23, *23*

ARMSTRONG HOUSE, Indiana 68

ARNOLD HOUSE, Wisconsin 186

AULDBRASS PLANTATION, South Carolina 173

AUSTIN HOUSE, South Carolina 173

BACH HOUSE, Illinois 76–77, *76*

BAGLEY HOUSE, Illinois 82–83

BAGLEY SUMMER HOUSE, Michigan 130

BAIRD HOUSE, Massachusetts 127

BAKER HOUSE, Illinois 90, *90*

BALCH HOUSE, Illinois 87, *87*

BALDWIN HOUSE, Illinois 83

BARNSDALL HOUSE, *12,* 12, 17, 32, 42, *54–59,* 208–212, *209*

BARTON HOUSE, New York *152–153,* 154, *154, 155*

BASSETT HOUSE REMODELING, Oak Park, Illinois 247

BAZETT HOUSE, California 34, 38, *50–51,*

BEACHY HOUSE, Illinois 86, *86*

BERGER HOUSE, California 34, 44, *44*

BETH SHALOM SYNAGOGUE, Pennsylvania 17, *168–169,* 170, *170,* 171, 221, *222–223*

BLAIR HOUSE, Wyoming 195

BLOSSOM GARAGE, Illinois 76

BLOSSOM HOUSE, Illinois 72, 76, *106*

BOGK HOUSE, Wisconsin 188–189

BOOMER HOUSE, Arizona 24

BOOTH HOUSE, Illinois 81, *81*

BOSWELL HOUSE, Ohio 163

BOTT HOUSE, Missouri 140

BOULTER HOUSE, Ohio 163

BRADLEY HOUSE, Illinois 9, 72, 83

BRANDES HOUSE, Washington 183

BRAUNER HOUSE, Michigan 132

BRIDGE COTTAGE, Michigan 127

BRIGHAM HOUSE, Illinois 81

BROADACRE CITY 15, 34, 62, 128, 134

BROWN (CHARLES E.) HOUSE, Illinois 80

BROWN (ERIC V.) HOUSE, Michigan 130, *130, 133*

BROWNE'S BOOKSTORE, Illinois 246

BUEHLER HOUSE, California 34, 42

BUFFALO EXPOSITION PAVILION, New York 248

BULBULIAN HOUSE, Minnesota 137

CARLSON HOUSE, Arizona 24

CARNEGIE MUSEUM OF ART, Pennsylvania 170

CARR HOUSE, Illinois 82

CARR SUMMER HOUSE, Michigan 130

CASS HOUSE ("CRIMSON BEECH"), New York 156

CHAHROUDI HOUSE, New York 155

CHARNLEY HOUSE, Illinois 8, *8, 72,* 75, *108, 109,*

CHARNLEY SUMMER HOUSE AND GUESTHOUSE, Mississippi 144

CHENEY HOUSE, Illinois 74, 87, *97, 104, 105*

CHRISTIAN HOUSE, Indiana 69

CHRISTIE HOUSE, New Jersey 150

CITY NATIONAL BANK HOUSE, Iowa 112, *112–113,* 114

COMO ORCHARD SUMMER COLONY, Montana 145, 246, 248

COOK HOUSE, Texas 174, 175

COOKE HOUSE, Virginia 180

COONLEY HOUSE, Illinois 90, *90, 110*

COONLEY PRIVATE PLAYHOUSE HOUSE, Illinois 89, *89*

COPELAND HOUSE, Illinois 69, 86

"CRIMSON BEECH" (CASS HOUSE), New York 156

CUMMINGS REAL ESTATE OFFICE, Illinois 248

DANA-THOMAS HOUSE, Illinois 72, 91, *91, 92–93,* 202, *204–205,* 207–208, *226–231*

DAVENPORT HOUSE, Illinois 72, 89

DAVIDSON HOUSE, New York 154, *156–157*

DAVIS HOUSE, Indiana 68

DeCARO HOUSE, Illinois 86, *96*

DELEVAN LAKE GROUP, Wisconsin 187

DeRHODES HOUSE, Indiana 68–69

E-Z POLISH FACTORY AND OFFICES, Illinois 78, *78*

"EAGLEFEATHER" (OBOLER RETREAT), California 32

EDWARDS HOUSE, Michigan 132

ELAY HOUSE, Minnesota 135

EMMOND HOUSE, Illinois 72, 84, *84*

ENNIS HOUSE, California *13,* 34, 39, 40, *41, 42, 210, 211,* 212, *238, 239*

EPPSTEIN HOUSE, Michigan 129

ERDMAN PREFABS, 74, 134, 135, 152, 186

EUCHTMAN HOUSE, Maryland 126

EVANS HOUSE, Illinois 76

FABYAN HOUSE, Illinois *72, 73,* 80

"FALLINGWATER" (EDGAR KAUFMANN HOUSE), Pennsylvania 15, 17, 85, *168–169,* 170

FASBENDER MEDICAL CLINIC, Minnesota *134–135,* 136

FAWCETT HOUSE, California 34, 42

FEIMAN HOUSE, Ohio 162

FELDMAN HOUSE, California 36

FIRST CHRISTIAN CHURCH, Arizona *20, 21,* 23

FIRST NATIONAL BANK (SMITH BANK), Illinois 80, *81*

"FIR TREE" (FREEMAN SUMMER HOUSE), New Mexico 150

FLORIDA SOUTHERN COLLEGE, Florida *60,* 64, *63–67,* 224, *225, 244, 245*

FLW FIELD OFFICE, Pennsylvania 170, *172*

FOSTER HOUSE, Illinois 76

"FOUNTAINHEAD" (HUGHES HOUSE), Mississippi 144

FOX RIVER COUNTRY CLUB, Illinois 247

FRANCIS APARTMENTS, Illinois 246

FRANCISCO TERRACE APARTMENTS, Illinois 246

FREDRICK HOUSE, Illinois 74

FREEMAN HOUSE, California 34, 38

FREEMAN SUMMER HOUSE ("FIR TREE"), New Mexico 150

FRICKE HOUSE, Illinois *71,* 85–86, *101*

FRIEDMAN (ALLEN) HOUSE, Illinois 74

FRIEDMAN (SOL) HOUSE, New York 155

FULLER (GRACE) HOUSE, Illinois 247

FULLER (WELBIE) HOUSE, Mississippi 248

FURBECK HOUSE, Illinois 85, 87, *87*

GALE (MRS. THOMAS H.) HOUSE, Illinois 85, 246

GALE (MRS. THOMAS H.) SUMMER HOUSES, Michigan 133

GALE (THOMAS H.) HOUSE, Illinois 85

GALE (THOMAS H.) SUMMER HOUSES, Michigan 133

GALE (WALTER H.) HOUSE, Illinois 72, 85, *85*

GALESBERG COUNTRY HOMES, Michigan 128

GENEVA INN, Wisconsin 249

GERMAN WAREHOUSE, Wisconsin 184, 190, *195*

GERTS COTTAGE, Michigan 248

GERTS DUPLEX, Michigan 133

GILLIN HOUSE, Texas 174, 175

GILMORE HOUSE ("AIRPLANE HOUSE"), Wisconsin 188

GLASNER HOUSE, Illinois 81, *81*

GLORE HOUSE, Illinois 83, *83*
GOAN HOUSE, Illinois 84
GODDARD HOUSE, Michigan 132
GOETSCH-WINCKLER HOUSE, Michigan 132
GOODRICH HOUSE, Illinois 87–88, *100*
GORDON HOUSE, Oregon 166
GRADY GAMMAGE MEMORIAL AUDITORIUM, Arizona 22, *24*, 25, *25*
GRANT HOUSE, Iowa 114
"GRAYCLIFF" (MARTIN SUMMER HOUSE), New York 152
GREENBERG HOUSE ("STONEBROKE"), Wisconsin 186
GREENE HOUSE, Illinois 74, *74*
GRIDLEY HOUSE, Illinois 75, *75*
GRIGGS HOUSE, Washington 183
GUGGENHEIM MUSEUM, New York 15, 16, 17, 34, *151*, 152, 155, *160, 161*, 218, 224, *224*

HAGAN HOUSE, Pennsylvania 170
HANNA HOUSE ("HONEYCOMB" HOUSE), California 17, *32–33*, 34, 48
HARDY HOUSE, Wisconsin 190
"HAREM" (THOMAS HOUSE), Illinois *71*, 72, 86
HARLAN HOUSE, Illinois 246
HARPER HOUSE, Michigan 133
HEATH HOUSE, New York 154, *158*
HELLER HOUSE, Illinois 78–79, *78–79*
HENDERSON HOUSE, Illinois 80
HEURTLEY HOUSE, Illinois 86, *96–97, 100, 111*
HEURTLEY SUMMER HOUSE, Michigan 131
HICKOX HOUSE, Illinois 9, 72, 83
HILLS/DECARO HOUSE, Illinois 86, *96*
"HILLSIDE" (PRICE, JR. HOUSE), Oklahoma 166
HILLSIDE HOME SCHOOL, Wisconsin 249
HOFFMAN AUTO SHOWROOM, New York 155
HOFFMAN HOUSE, New York 157
"HOLLYHOCK" HOUSE (BARNSDALL HOUSE), *12*, 12, 17, 32, 42, *54–59*, 208–212, *209, 234–237*
HOME AND STUDIO, Illinois17, 70, 72, 85, *94, 95*, 196, *196, 197*, 198, *199, 200, 201*, 202, *202, 203*, 206, 253
"HONEYCOMB" HOUSE (HANNA HOUSE), 17, *32–33*,
HORNER HOUSE, Illinois 246
HORSE SHOW FOUNTAIN, Illinois *111*
HORSESHOE INN, Colorado 246
HOTEL PLAZA APARTMENT REMODELING, New York 248
HOYT HOUSE, Illinois 80, *80, 81*
HUGHES HOUSE ("FOUNTAINHEAD"), Mississippi 144
HUNT HOUSE (FIRST), Illinois 84, *84*
HUNT HOUSE (SECOND), Wisconsin 189
HUSSER HOUSE, Illinois 246

IBER HOUSE, Wisconsin 192
IMPERIAL HOTEL, Japan 6, 10, 12, 13, 170, 249
INGALLS HOUSE, Illinois 89, *89*
IRVING HOUSE, Illinois 79

JACKSON HOUSE ("SKYVIEW"), Wisconsin 188
JACOBS HOUSE (FIRST), Wisconsin 15, 34, 186, 188
JACOBS HOUSE (SECOND), Wisconsin 188
JOHNSON & SON ADMINISTRATION BUILDING AND RESEARCH TOWER, Wisconsin (JOHNSON'S WAX BUILDING) *15*, 15, 17, 186, *186, 187*, 190, *190*, *216, 217*, 218–221, *218*
JOHNSON (A.P.) HOUSE, Wisconsin 187
JOHNSON (HERBERT F.) HOUSE ("WINGSPREAD"), Wisconsin 186, 190, 194
JOHNSON (KAREN) HOUSE, Wisconsin 190
JONES (FRED B.) HOUSE ("PENWERN"), Wisconsin 187
JONES (RICHARD LLOYD) HOUSE ("WESTHOPE"), Oklahoma 15, 164, 166, *166*
JUVENILE CULTURAL STUDY CENTER, Kansas 120–123, *120–121*

KALIL HOUSE, New Hampshire 146, *146–147*
KALITA HUMPHREYS THEATER, Texas 174, *174–175*, 176, *176, 177, 220*, 221
KANSAS CITY COMMUNITY CHRISTIAN CHURCH, Missouri 140, *141, 142–143*, 221
KAUFMANN HOUSE, Pennsylvania 15, 17, 85, 168–169, 170
KAUFMANN OFFICE, VICTORIA AND ALBERT MUSEUM, London 6, 170, 218, 248
KEYS HOUSE, Minnesota 137
KIER HOUSE, Illinois *80*, 81
KINNEY (STERLING) HOUSE, Texas 174, 175
KINNEY (PATRICK) HOUSE, Wisconsin 187
KISSAM HOUSE, Illinois *72*, 80
KRAUS HOUSE, Missouri 140
KUNDERT MEDICAL CLINIC, California 45
KUNDERT MEDICAL CLINIC, Montana 145

"LA MINIATURA"(ALICE MILLARD HOUSE), California 34, 42–44, *42*
LAMBERSON HOUSE, Iowa 116
LAMP HOUSE, Wisconsin 1880
LAMP HOUSE, Wisconsin 249
LARKIN COMPANY ADMINISTRATION BUILDING, New York 10, 218, 248
LAURENT HOUSE, Illinois 90
LEVIN HOUSE, Michigan 131
LEWIS (GEORGE) HOUSE, Florida 66
LEWIS (LLOYD) HOUSE, Illinois 84
LINDHOLM HOUSE, Minnesota 135
LINDHOLM SERVICE STATION, Minnesota 136, *136*

LITTLE HOUSE (FIRST), Illinois 88
LITTLE HOUSE (SECOND), Minnesota 170, 248
LOVNESS HOUSE AND COTTAGE, Minnesota 137, *137, 138, 139*, 212
LYKES HOUSE, Arizona 22, 24

MACBEAN HOUSE, Minnesota 137
MANSON HOUSE, Wisconsin 194
MARDEN HOUSE, Virginia 178, 180
MARIN COUNTY CIVIC CENTER, California *17*, 17, 34, 45–48, *45, 46–47*
MARSHALL ERDMAN PREFABS, 74, 134, 135, 152, 186
MARTIN (DWIGHT D.) GARDENER'S COTTAGE, New York 155, *159*
MARTIN (WILLIAM E.) HOUSE, Illinois 88, *88*
MARTIN (DWIGHT D.) HOUSE, New York 154
MARTIN (DWIGHT D.) SUMMER HOUSE AND GARAGE, New York 155
MATHEWS HOUSE, California 36,
MAY HOUSE, Michigan 130, *131*
MCARTHUR HOUSE AND STABLE, Illinois 76
MCCARTNEY HOUSE, Michigan 130, *130*
MCHARG HOUSE, Illinois 246
MEIJA MURA, Japan 170
METROPOLITAN MUSEUM OF ART, New York 170, 248
MEYER HOUSE, Michigan 129
MIDWAY GARDENS, Illinois 11, 246
MILLARD (ALICE) HOUSE ("LA MINIATURA"), California 34
MILLARD (GEORGE) HOUSE, Illinois 82, *99*
MILLER HOUSE, Iowa 114
MOLLICA HOUSE, Wisconsin 186
MOORE HOUSE, Illinois 86, *107*
MORI ORIENTAL ART STUDIO, Illinois 246
MORRIS GIFT SHOP, California 17, 34, 45
MOSSBERG HOUSE, Indiana 68
MUELLER HOUSE, Illinois 79
MUNICIPAL BOATHOUSE, Wisconsin 249
MUNKWITZ DUPLEX APARTMENTS, Wisconsin 249
MYERS MEDICAL CLINIC, Ohio 163

NEILS HOUSE, Minnesota 136
NEW YORK CITY EXHIBITION, New York 248
NICHOLS HOUSE, Illinois 80

OAK PARK, Illinois 8, 17, 70, *71*, 74, 85–88, 112, 184, 196, 198, 200, 202, 246
OBOLER GATEHOUSE AND RETREAT, California 34, 42, *43*
OCOTILLO CAMP, Arizona 14, 246
OLFELT HOUSE, Minnesota 137

PALMER HOUSE, Michigan 128
PAPPAS HOUSE, Missouri 140
PARK RIDGE COUNTRY CLUB REMODELING,

Illinois 248
PARKER HOUSE, Illinois 85
PARKWYN VILLAGE, Michigan 128, 130, 131
PEARCE HOUSE, California 38
PEBBLES & BALCH SHOP, Oak Park, Illinois 248
PENFIELD HOUSE, Ohio 163
"PENWERN" (JONES HOUSE), Wisconsin 187
PERRY HOUSE, Illinois 82
PETERSEN COTTAGE, Wisconsin 187, *188*, *189*
PETTIT MEMORIAL CHAPEL, Illinois 75, *98*, *99*
PEW HOUSE, Wisconsin 190
PIEPER HOUSE, Arizona 20, 22,
PILGRIM CONGREGATIONAL CHURCH, California 44, *52*, *53*
POPE-LEIGHEY HOUSE, Virginia 178, *178–179*, 180, *180*, 181, *182*, 212–216, *214–215*, 240
PORTER HOUSE ("TANYDERI"), Wisconsin 190
POST HOUSE, Illinois 74
PRATT HOUSE, Michigan 129
PRICE COMPANY TOWER, Oklahoma *17*, 17, 164, *164–165*, *167*, 220, 221, *242*, *243*
PRICE, JR. HOUSE ("HILLSIDE"), Oklahoma 166
PRICE, SR. HOUSE, Arizona 22

RAVINE BLUFFS DEVELOPMENT, Illinois 74, 80, 81, 82, *82*
RAYWARD HOUSE, Connecticut 60
REBHUHN HOUSE, New York 152, 155
REISLEY HOUSE, New York 156
RICHARDS BUNGALOW, Wisconsin 189, *191*
RICHARDS DUPLEX APARTMENTS, Wisconsin 189
RICHARDS SMALL HOUSE, Wisconsin 189
RICHARDSON HOUSE, New Jersey 150
RIVER FOREST GOLF CLUB, Illinois 9, 248
RIVER FOREST TENNIS CLUB, Illinois 89, *89*
RIVER FOREST, Illinois, 9, 72, 89
RIVERVIEW TERRACE RESTAURANT ("THE SPRING GREEN"), Wisconsin 192–194
ROBERTS (ABBY BEECHER) HOUSE, Michigan 131
ROBERTS (CHARLES) HOUSE, Illinois 87
ROBERTS (ISABEL) HOUSE, Illinois 89, *97*
ROBIE HOUSE, Illinois 17, 72, 74, 79, 79
ROLOSON APARTMENTS, Illinois 75
ROMEO AND JULIET WINDMILL, 9, 186, 191, *191*
ROOKERY BUILDING OFFICE ENTRANCE AND LOBBY, Illinois 77
ROOT HOUSE, Illinois 81
ROSENBAUM HOUSE, Alabama 18, *18*, *19*, 212, *241*
ROSS (WILLIAM F.) HOUSE, Illinois 80

ROSS (CHARLES S.) HOUSE, Wisconsin 187
RUBIN HOUSE, Ohio 162–163
RUDIN HOUSE, Wisconsin 188

SAN MARCOS-IN-THE-DESERT, Arizona 14
SANDER HOUSE, Connecticut 60
SCHABERG HOUSE, Michigan 132
SCHULTZ HOUSE, Michigan 133
SCHWARTZ HOUSE, Wisconsin 194
SERLIN HOUSE, New York 155
SHAVIN HOUSE, Tennessee 173
"SKYVIEW" (JACKSON HOUSE), Wisconsin 188
SMITH (RICHARD) HOUSE, Wisconsin 186
SMITH BANK (FIRST NATIONAL BANK), Illinois 80, *81*
SMITH (GEORGE W.) HOUSE, Illinois 86–87, *86*
SMITH (MELVIN) HOUSE, Michigan 127, 128
"SNOWFLAKE" (WALL HOUSE), Michigan 132
SONDERN HOUSE, Missouri 140
SOUTHERN COLLEGE, Florida *60*, 64, *63–67*, 224, *225*, *244*, *245*
SPENCER (DUDLEY) HOUSE, Delaware 60
SPENCER (GEORGE W.) HOUSE, Wisconsin 187
"SPRING GREEN" (RIVERVIEW TERRACE RESTAURANT), Wisconsin 192–194
STALEY HOUSE, Ohio 163
STEFFENS HOUSE, Illinois 246
STEWART HOUSE, California 32, 42
STOCKMAN HOUSE, Iowa 112, 114, *115*
STOHR ARCADE BUILDING, Illinois 247
"STONEBROKE" (GREENBERG HOUSE), Wisconsin 186
STORER HOUSE, California 34, 38, *38*
STROMQUIST HOUSE, Utah 177
STURGES HOUSE, California 34, 38, *48*, *49*,
SULLIVAN HOUSE, Illinois 247
SULLIVAN SUMMER HOUSE AND STABLES, Mississippi 144
SUNDAY HOUSE, Iowa 114
SUNTOP HOMES, Pennsylvania 169, 170
SUTTON HOUSE, Nebraska 145
SWEETON HOUSE, New Jersey 150

TALIESIN EAST *10,*
TALIESIN FELLOWSHIP COMPLEX, Wisconsin 192
TALIESIN VISITORS CENTER, Wisconsin 192
TALIESIN WEST, Arizona 15, 16, *16*, 17, 20, 22, 26, *26–31*, 184, 208, *209*, *232–233*, 246, *253*
TALIESIN, SPRING GREEN, Wisconsin 11, 12, 13, 14, 17, 72, 184, 186, 191–193, *192*, *193*
TALIESIN, Wisconsin 249

TEATER STUDIO, Idaho 68
THOMAS HOUSE ("HAREM"), Illinois *71*, 86
THURBER ART GALLERY, Illinois 247
TOMEK HOUSE, Illinois 90
TONKENS HOUSE, Ohio 162
TRACY HOUSE, Washington 183
TRIER HOUSE, Iowa 114
TURKEL HOUSE, Michigan 127, 128

UNITARIAN MEETING HOUSE, Wisconsin 17, *185*, 186, 190
UNITY TEMPLE, Illinois 17, 74, 87, *102*, *103*, 112
USONIA HOMES, New York 154, 155, 156, 162

VAN TAMELEN HOUSE, Wisconsin 188
VICTORIA AND ALBERT MUSEUM, London 6, 170, 218
VOSBERG SUMMER HOUSE, Michigan 130

WALKER HOUSE, California 34, 38, *38*
WALL HOUSE ("SNOWFLAKE"), Michigan 132
WALLER APARTMENTS, Illinois 246
WALLER APARTMENTS, Illinois 78, *79*
WALLER HOUSE REMODELING, Illinois 248
WALLIS SUMMER HOUSE, Wisconsin 187
WALSER HOUSE, Illinois 76
WALTER HOUSE, Iowa 114, 116, *116–117*, 212, *213*, 218, 240
WALTER RIVER PAVILION, Iowa 116, *117–118*
WALTON HOUSE, California 34, 42, *42*, *43*
WEISBLAT HOUSE, Michigan 129
WELTZHEIMER HOUSE, Ohio 162, 163
WESTCOTT HOUSE, Ohio 162, 163
"WESTHOPE" (JONES HOUSE), Oklahoma 15, 164, 166, *166*
WILLEY HOUSE, Minnesota 134, 136
WILLIAMS HOUSE, Illinois *88*, 89
WILLITS HOUSE, Illinois 9, 17, 72, 82, *82*, *83*
WILSON HOUSE, New Jersey 150
"WINGSPREAD" (HERBERT F. JOHNSON HOUSE), Wisconsin 186, 190, 194
WINN HOUSE, Michigan 131
WINSLOW HOUSE, Illinois 9, 17, 72, 89
WOOLLEY HOUSE, Illinois 88
WRIGHT (DAVID) HOUSE, Arizona 22,
WRIGHT (DUEY) HOUSE, Wisconsin 194
WRIGHT (ROBERT LLEWELLYN), Maryland 126
WYOMING VALLEY JUNIOR SCHOOL, Wisconsin 194

YOUNG HOUSE, Illinois 87

ZIEGLER HOUSE, Kentucky 126
ZIMMERMAN HOUSE, New Hampshire 146, *147*, *148–149*, 212, *213*, 213, 217–218, *216*

ROMEO AND JULIET

"ROMEO AND
JULIET WILL
STAND 25 YEARS
WHICH IS LONGER
THAN THE IRON
TOWERS STAND
AROUND THERE.
I AM AFRAID ALL
OF MY UNCLES
THEMSELVES MAY
BE GONE BEFORE
ROMEO AND
JULIET. LET'S GO."

**Wright's daring design
for the Romeo and Juliet
tower (right) gave notice
of his determination to
test the boundaries of
architectural design and
engineering as early as
the 1890s.**

One of Frank Lloyd Wright's early forays into tradition-defying design was a windmill for his aunts, Jane and Nell Lloyd Jones. When their brothers objected to the unconventional tower and warned against building it, Wright persuaded the aunts to stand firm. Romeo and Juliet survived his modest prediction four times over and endures as a symbol of the architect's confident spirit.

It all began in 1896 when Wright's aunts were in the market for a windmill that would complement the look of the school buildings Wright had designed for them ten years earlier. Wright, then age 29, proposed a bold design based on two interlocking forms—a taller, diamond shaped structure, named "Romeo," and an octagonal form named "Juliet." This interlocking construction gave the 60-foot windmill strength to stand without the aid of internal cross supports. Romeo became the "storm prow" that faced off harsh winter winds sending them safely around Juliet. Jane and Nell were overjoyed at the tower's beauty, but Wright's uncles, who favored a standard metal tripod mill, claimed it was too expensive and would come down in the first big storm. Despite the cost and ornery warnings, the aunts put their faith in nephew Frank and the windmill was built. Though it no longer pumps water, Romeo and Juliet stands upright and strong to this day, "rooted as the trees." ■

The southwestern
Wisconsin landscape
stayed with Wright
wherever he traveled.
Among his fondest images
of home was the way
classic red barns dotted
the hillsides. With
Midway, he created
one of his own.

MIDWAY FARM

"A FARMSTEAD HERE IS SOMEHOW WARMED AND GIVEN LIFE BY THE RED OF
THE BARNS AS THEY STAND ABOUT ME OVER THE GREEN HILLS AND AMONG
THE YELLOW FIELDS WITH THE SUN ON THEM."

When Wright was a boy, the hill-sides near Spring Green, Wisconsin, were dotted with farms belonging to his Lloyd Jones uncles. Wright's own interest in farming and his desire to create a self-sustaining country dwelling prompted him to build barns, a chicken house and horse stables adjacent to his home, Taliesin, in 1911.

In the 1930s, with the arrival of the Taliesin Fellowship, Wright decided to move the farming operation from Taliesin to a low, round hill midway between Taliesin and Hillside School. A farm cottage and a tall horse barn once belonging to his Uncle John were moved up to the slope. With that as the basis, Wright created a series of long, horizontal farm buildings that would serve as dairy, calf barn and granary. At the end of the barn he built a limestone turret with a spire on top to serve as the milk house.

By 1947, Midway Farm was complete and fully operational. The raising of calves, chickens and pigs, the plowing and planting of nearby fields, all became part of the Taliesin Fellowship experience. ∎

The spire of the creamery at Midway makes a strong vertical statement amidst Wright's horizontal farm buildings.

also included a gymnasium, science lab, art studio and classrooms. Hillside School closed in 1915 and the building remained idle until 1932, the height of the Great Depression.

Although at the time he had few commissions, the 65-year-old Wright gave no thought to retirement. Instead he began a new phase of creativity by founding the Taliesin Fellowship, a school for apprentice architects. With his wife Olgivanna, Wright planned the training program that would be based, much as his aunts' school had been, on a system of "learning by doing."

Twenty-three apprentices answered the call that first year and practical lessons began immediately. With the apprentices' enthusiastic help, Wright remodeled Hillside Home School, adding a large drafting studio and dormitory wing and converting the school's gymnasium into a theater.

As with Taliesin and other buildings on the vast estate, Wright couldn't leave Hillside alone. He remodeled and changed it throughout his life. A fire in 1952 gave Wright the chance to move the Taliesin Fellowship dining room from Taliesin to Hillside and completely revise the theater. ■

Openess and light flood the Hillside dining room (left). In the assembly hall at Hillside (above), Wright did away with the "box" to create a room of infinite space.

The theater at Hillside is an intimate space for music, dance and dramatic performances. The stage curtain, designed by Wright, is an abstract landscape of his ancestral valley.

HERE IS THE TEST OF WISDOM .... WISDOM IS NOT FINALLY TESTED IN SCHOOLS .... WISDOM CANNOT BE PASSED FROM ONE HAVING IT TO ANOTHER NOT HAVING IT .... WISDOM IS OF THE SOUL .. IS NOT SUSCEPTIBLE OF PROOF .. IS ITS OWN PROOF .. APPLIES TO ALL OBJECTS .. STAGES AND QUALITIES .. IS CONTENT .. WISDOM IS THE CERTAINTY OF THE REALITY & IMMORTALITY OF THINGS .. AND THE EXCELLENCE OF THINGS .. SOMETHING THERE IS IN THE FLOAT OF THE SIGHT OF THINGS THAT PROVOKES IT OUT OF THE SOUL ..

WALT WHITMAN

This 5000-square-foot drafting studio was the primary addition to Hillside in 1932 when the Taliesin Fellowship was formed. Inside, Wright's "abstract forest" of oak triangle columns support large oak trusses with exposed cross beams.

HILLSIDE

"ARCHITECTURE, I HAVE LEARNED, IS NO LESS A

WEAVING OF FABRIC THAN THE TREES."

Hillside Home School (above), constructed of indigenous sandstone from quarries a mile away and oak from nearby woods, has a strong, quiet character that reflects Wright's Welsh heritage.

F rank Lloyd Wright designed Hillside Home School in 1902 for his aunts, Jane and Nell Lloyd Jones, who ran one of the nation's first co-educational boarding schools. This was the second building Wright designed for them on the site. The first, an 1887 shingle-style building, was demolished by Wright in the 1950s.

It was at Hillside Home School, in the large assembly hall, that Wright said he first attempted to break the boxlike, Victorian rooms popular at the turn of the century. In this impressive two-story room the walls seem to vanish as the space flows both vertically and horizontally. The structure, built of native oak and ashlar-cut sandstone,

set close beneath deep eaves, bring sunlight into every room at some time during the day.

Twice, in 1914 and 1925, Taliesin was damaged by fire. Each time Wright rebuilt, determined to make the next incarnation better than the last. As a design created for himself rather than a client, Taliesin allowed him to possess it completely and change it constantly. Wright spent nearly 50 years working on Taliesin. He didn't stop adding to it or changing it until the day he died.

Although Wright traveled much during his lifetime, Taliesin continued to pull him back. "Taliesin! When I am away from it, like some rubber band stretched out but ready to snap back (when) the pull is relaxed or released, I get back to it, happy to be home again." ■

© 1995 PEDRO GUERRERO

Flower-filled courtyards and graceful walkways (left) make Taliesin a natural companion to the earth. Frank Lloyd Wright's personal study at Taliesin (above) has the intimate feel of familiar objects. Natural light washes in from three sides and a skylight.

© 1995 ERIC OXENDORF

The two-story height of the room that served as Wright's home studio at Taliesin made full use of natural light from a large bank of north-facing windows. From this studio Wright created many of his most well-known architectural works.

TALIESIN

"ITS ELEVATION FOR ME...IS THE MODELING OF THE HILLS, THE WEAVING AND THE FABRIC THAT CLINGS TO THEM, THE LOOK OF IT ALL IN TENDER GREEN OR COVERED WITH SNOW OR IN FULL GLOW OF SUMMER THAT BURSTS INTO THE GLORIOUS BLAZE OF AUTUMN."

Described as the greatest domestic space in America, the living room at Taliesin (below) illustrates **Wright's** ability to combine simple materials into elegant forms.

Frank Lloyd Wright considered Taliesin to be the supreme "natural house." He said the many-leveled home blended so completely with its native surroundings that "it was not so easy to tell where pavements and walls left off and ground began."

Wright was 44 years old in 1911 when he returned to the valley of his childhood to build his "house of the north." Spread over 37,000 square feet, this self-sufficient country dwelling included living quarters, an office, drafting studio, guest rooms, farm buildings, stables, an ice house and various other structures. Orchards, berry patches, kitchen gardens, courtyards and a water-garden completed the scene.

Wright chose native yellow limestone quarried nearby as the basic building material for Taliesin and devised a method of laying up the stone that simulated the stratified layers in which it was found naturally. Inside, the sand-colored plaster walls are trimmed in cypress and floors are made of waxed cypress boards or stone. Bands of windows,

© 1995 ERIC OXENDORF

Steel beams recovered from a World War II aircraft carrier provide support for the soaring Birdwalk. Added to Taliesin in 1953, this unique balcony provides a matchless view of the valley and, looking back, a rare perspective on the house itself.

Frank Lloyd Wright worked into his 90s and often could be found in the drafting studio at Hillside (left) preparing drawings for a current commission. The Lloyd Jones family sat for this portrait (below) in 1883 with patriarch Richard beside a chair left vacant in memory of his late wife. Young Frank is seated to the right of the empty chair with his sister on his lap.

Some 20 years after he began building Taliesin, Wright founded the Taliesin Fellowship, a training program for young architects. To accommodate the group, Wright enlarged Hillside, adding a drafting studio and living quarters. The farm operation, run by the Fellowship, eventually was moved from the house to Midway Farm, a series of low, red buildings situated "midway" between Taliesin and Hillside.

Taliesin was Wright's principal residence until his death in 1959. The buildings are used now much as they were in Wright's day, with Taliesin Architects and apprentices of the Frank Lloyd Wright School of Architecture working side by side in the great drafting studio. Resident members of the school and firm, some of whom worked with Wright, continue to live on site forming an active community of architects and artists.

The Taliesin property achieved National Historic Landmark status in 1976. In 1990 the Taliesin Preservation Commission was formed to work with the Frank Lloyd Wright Foundation in preserving Taliesin for future generations and conduct tours of the site.

Frank Lloyd Wright overlooked nothing in his design of Taliesin and he had the luxury of years to rework it again and again. The photographs that follow capture the work of his lifetime and help explain why Wright cast such a long shadow in 20th-Century art and architecture. ■

Taliesin's horizontal lines allow it to settle naturally along the hillside Wright chose for his home, the longest ongoing project of his career.

Wright's own connection to the valley surrounding Taliesin goes back to the mid-1800s when his Welsh ancestors, the Lloyd Jones family, homesteaded the area near the Wisconsin River and the village of Spring Green. During summers spent on his uncle's farm, the young Wright learned to appreciate the patterns and rhythms of nature he found in the branch of a tree, outcroppings of limestone or the ever-shifting sandbars along the river. Wright's basic concepts of "organic architecture" were born then. He later advised his apprentices to "study nature, love nature, stay close to nature. It will never fail you."

The future architect came to love one hillside in particular where he picked spring flowers as a boy. Wright realized, instinctively, that any structure built on a hill would destroy it. "It should be of the hill, belonging to it, so hill and house could live together each the happier for the other."

When it came to positioning a house on this hill, Wright treated the building as an element of nature. Taliesin's many wings and terraces reach out along the crest or "brow" of the hill, embracing rather than commanding the site. In the Welsh tradition, Wright gave his home a name, one

that captured exactly the impression he was after: the word *Taliesin* (tally eh sin) means "shining brow."

In 1911, as Wright began building Taliesin, earlier works, designed for the family, were already in evidence. Hillside Home School of 1902 and the controversial Romeo and Juliet tower of 1896, both designed for his aunts, stood to the south. Tan-y-deri House, created for his sister in 1907, was across the valley. And in the near distance sat Unity Chapel, the Lloyd Jones "cottage church" for which Wright is said to have designed the interiors.

TALIESIN
THE WORK OF A LIFETIME

A long a quiet county road in southwestern Wisconsin, there is a
stretch of hill and valley that catches
the eye and holds it. As the landscape goes
full to the horizon, hidden details can be
glimpsed. A flash of low roof or stately
spire. The unmistakably simple lines of a
long red barn. The fleeting reflection of
sunlit stone walls. This is Taliesin, country
home of Frank Lloyd Wright, the most celebrated of American architects. And this is
the place, beyond all others, where Wright
designed and built and experimented freely
with the ideas that have so invigorated the
worlds of art and architecture.

Taliesin was more than a house to Frank
Lloyd Wright. This low, wooded hillside
became the most inspirational workshop of
his life. Today, structures from every
decade of his career are found on the 600-
acre site, making Taliesin the rarest single
collection of Wright's work anywhere in
the world. His earliest effort, a family
chapel built in 1886 is here, as are more
mature designs of the 1950s. The house
itself has been praised by generations of
architects, historians and critics as a triumph of design. Taliesin stands now as the
truest record of what Wright thought, how
he worked and how he lived.

TALIESIN

"I FEEL MY ROOTS IN THESE HILLSIDES . . ."

FRANK LLOYD WRIGHT ®

TAN-Y-DERI

Frank Lloyd Wright's early residential designs are represented at Taliesin by Tan-y-deri, a house he designed in 1907 for his sister Jane and her family. Tan-y-deri is Welsh for "under the oaks," a reference to its placement on a wooded rise. Indeed, the two-story shingled house commands one of the best views of Wright's own house, Taliesin. Tan-y-deri retains its original diamond-paned leaded glass windows which are framed on the inside by simple wooden banding. ■

Tan-y-deri House (left) displays the spreading roof with deep over-hangs that Wright would use in many future designs. Three simple rooms make up Unity Chapel (below), an important gathering place for the Lloyd Jones family when first built.

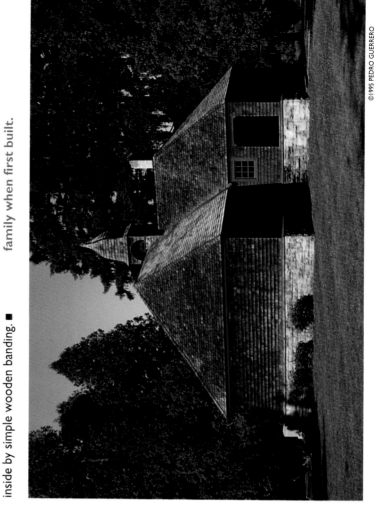

UNITY CHAPEL

Their Unitarian faith inspired the Lloyd Jones family to immigrate to the United States in the 1840s, eventually finding their the way to the area near Spring Green. In time, the family wanted their own building in which to worship and Unity Chapel was built. Unity Chapel (1886) was the first building in the valley in which Wright participated as a designer. Working at the time for Joseph L. Silsbee, a Chicago architect commissioned to create the "cottage church," Wright was assigned to supervise the interior, although it is speculated his involvement may have been greater. Unity Chapel remained important to Wright throughout his life. ■

17

WRIGHT'S LANDSCAPE

"ARCHITECTURE PROPERLY STUDIED IN RELATION TO THE NATURAL FEATURES SURROUNDING IT IS A GREAT CLARIFIER AND DEVELOPER OF THE BEAUTY OF THE LANDSCAPE."

nspired by nature when he wandered the valley as a boy, Wright learned to integrate its forms in all dimensions of his work. The swift Wisconsin River and the many tributaries that crossed his ancestor's farmsteads offered him the opportunity to include water as a major design component of Taliesin. Wright felt water gave a landscape definition and a sense of completion. Thus, his vision for Taliesin included ponds and pools and, spectacularly, a waterfall. The slopes, ridges and waterways of Taliesin became yet another canvas for him and one he worked with particular skill. ∎

Texture and depth are evident in Frank Lloyd Wright's waterfall (right) which echoes nature as it plunges into the small stream below Taliesin. At one time the waterfall powered a small hydroelectric plant, making Taliesin (below) the first house in the valley to have electricity.

FRANK LLOYD WRIGHT®
VISITOR CENTER

"THIS WISCONSIN VALLEY...
EVERY TIME I COME BACK
HERE IT IS WITH THE FEELING
THERE IS NOTHING ANYWHERE
BETTER THAN THIS IS."

©1995 ERIC OXENDORF

A cross the highway below Taliesin, the Wisconsin River continues past the Frank Lloyd Wright Visitor Center, a building designed by Wright in 1953 as a gateway for visitors to Taliesin. Wright planned to operate a restaurant or tea room there with his apprentices serving as cooks and waiters. Construction got underway in the mid-1950s, but Wright, diverted by other work, did not live to see the building finished. In the 1960s the site was purchased and the building was completed as the Spring Green Restaurant. In its heyday, the restaurant was celebrated for both its Wright design and striking river view. In 1993, the building was purchased by the Taliesin Preservation Commission to become the Frank Lloyd Wright Visitor Center. With its bookstore, cafe and special exhibits on the master's work, the building now serves as the gateway Wright once envisioned. ■

The long, low Visitor Center design is true to Wright's determination to blend his buildings into the land. A 1993 interior renovation made way for a bookstore, cafe and exhibit area.

©1995 PEDRO GUERRERO